1977/78

1977/78

A Historic Season for
Rangers FC and a Treble
That Ended an Era

David Herd

First published by Pitch Publishing, 2023

Pitch Publishing
9 Donnington Park,
85 Birdham Road,
Chichester,
West Sussex,
PO20 7AJ
www.pitchpublishing.co.uk
info@pitchpublishing.co.uk

© 2023, David Herd

Every effort has been made to trace the copyright.
Any oversight will be rectified in future editions at the
earliest opportunity by the publisher.

All rights reserved. No part of this book may be reproduced,
sold or utilised in any form or transmitted in any form or by
any means, electronic or mechanical, including photocopying,
recording or by any information storage and retrieval system,
without prior permission in writing from the Publisher.

A CIP catalogue record is available for this book
from the British Library.

ISBN 978 1 80150 449 2

Typesetting and origination by Pitch Publishing
Printed and bound in Great Britain by TJ Books, Padstow

Contents

Acknowledgements 9

Foreword 11

1. Pre-Season: New Faces 17

2. August: Unrest on the Terraces 26

3. September: The Comeback 43

4. October: The Team Hits Top Gear 62

5. November: John Greig MBE 87

6. December: An Unhappy Christmas 105

7. January: Old Firm Mayhem 116

8. February: The Battle of Fir Park 130

9. March: Tragedy and Triumph 149

10. April: A Captain's Tale 173

11. May: Treble Glory Then the End of an Era . . .203

Appendix: Full 1977/78 Competitive Results and Player Statistics 218

This book is dedicated to my good friend and former work colleague Gordon Brophy.

I truly hope we will see another European final together.

Acknowledgements

THIS IS my third Rangers book, and none of them would have been possible without the support and patience of my wife Diane. She has let me follow my dream, and I'm eternally grateful.

Since my writing career started at the ripe old age of 57, I have also received amazing encouragement and help from multiple Rangers fans, both groups and individuals. There are too many to name, but I do wish to especially thank Sie Leslie and Gordon Bond of The Gers TV, who gave me wonderful initial exposure by allowing me to speak at a dinner they had hosted at Ibrox Stadium to celebrate the 150th birthday of the club we all adore. Since then, I have recorded podcasts, written blogs, and become immersed in the online world of Rangers. I've also had the privilege of sharing a top table at speaking events with some great former players who I watched from the stands and terraces. Who knows what else I may get involved in as the years go on.

My thanks also go to Rangers FC who allowed the use of some images in this book.

Finally, I'd like to mention all the wonderful Rangers players who made season 1977/78 so memorable. It is a campaign that will always hold a special place in my affections. They were without doubt the favourite Rangers team of my younger days, and I look upon them even now as heroes. A special thank you to Alex MacDonald for providing the foreword and for giving his time so freely.

Sadly, too many of his team-mates mentioned in this book are no longer with us. To the memory of Ally Dawson, Bobby McKean, Colin Jackson, Davie Cooper, Johnny Hamilton, Sandy Jardine and Tom Forsyth. And, of course, to the men who built that wonderful team, the late great Willie Waddell and Jock Wallace, I raise a glass to absent friends.

Finally, the leader of that team, and the greatest captain I ever had the privilege of watching in a Rangers jersey, was 80 years old on 11 September 2022. John Greig MBE is the man given the ultimate accolade as The Greatest Ranger. If he ever reads this book, I sincerely hope he enjoys it.

Foreword

*by Alex MacDonald, Rangers FC
1968 to 1980*

I LIVED a boyhood dream to play for the club I always supported, right from the days when me and my best friend would climb into Ibrox Stadium from down near the railway line and have a kick about on the hallowed turf. In those days, the game only lasted until the groundsman chased us away. But in my 12 years as a Rangers player, that pitch became my home and I enjoyed so many great memories. Many of them were in season 1977/78, the subject of this book.

I was fortunate to play with so many fantastic players at Ibrox, and won three league titles, four Scottish Cups, four League Cups and, of course, the 1972 European Cup Winners' Cup. Two of those league titles were part of a treble, our team winning it twice in just three years. Season 1977/78 was the last of them, and we played some brilliant football along the way. There was no better performance than when we beat a very good Aberdeen team 6-1 in the League Cup, a match where I would say all ten outfield players played at the top of their game all at the same time. I managed to score that night with a header, not the last time I would do that against them that season.

Gordon Smith got a hat-trick against the Dons; he was one of three new players who all made a big impression. He was a quick and clever player and certainly mastered the art of the tap-in from three yards out! Davie Cooper also arrived from Clydebank, and what a skilful footballer he was. The last of the new men was my midfield partner for most of the season, young Bobby Russell. He had a great first season, and was a player who did the simple things really well. They joined a team that was a joy to play in, with Tommy McLean the man who made me look good in the air with the number of headers I scored from his crosses. Derek Johnstone up front scored even more of them, he was a great centre-half but an even better centre-forward. And, of course, there were the men behind me in defence. Tom Forsyth and Colin Jackson were wonderful defenders, John Greig was our leader on the park, and my great friend Sandy Jardine made up a back four that any team in the world would be happy with. Peter McCloy or Stewart Kennedy in goal were reliable and consistent no matter which one was picked.

Sandy and I remained close for many years, team-mates and room-mates, the best of friends. We were together at Hearts as well as at Rangers, and I still miss him. Too many of the players from that season are now gone. One of them was Bobby McKean, a great player who was so direct. His death was a tragedy, and it came just before we played Celtic in the League Cup Final. There was no better way to remember him than by winning the trophy, and it became the first leg of the treble when we won 2-1. It was a final we nearly never reached; we really struggled against Forfar in the semi-final, scoring late to take the game into extra time. I managed to score a 20-yarder as our fitness overpowered them after that.

FOREWORD

In the league, we had to beat Aberdeen to the title. They had some excellent players and would go on to win many trophies in the years to come. Probably the best win we had in the league was the day we beat Celtic 3-2 after being 2-0 down at half-time. The feeling at the final whistle that day was amazing, but the biggest thrill was when the whistle sounded at the end of our last game against Motherwell, as that meant we had won the title and I had my third championship medal. Ibrox was packed and we certainly enjoyed a good night afterwards.

The Scottish Cup was the final trophy, and I remember it started with a trip to Berwick ten years after Big Jock had played in goal when they knocked us out. There was a lot of pressure on us that day, but we managed to get through, and we beat a very good young team in Dundee United in the semi-final. They were another team who we could tell were going to improve, and every game against them was hard.

I had scored in the Scottish Cup Final against Hearts two years before when we had last won the treble, and I was lucky enough to score again against Aberdeen in the final as we took another treble back to Ibrox. It all started with Tommy McLean falling over the ball, as I like to remind him! It ended up getting to Bobby Russell, and I made his cross look good by diving to head it past Bobby Clark. Big Derek scored with another great header, and the cup was ours. We had no idea what was going on behind the scenes, but with Jock leaving a couple of weeks later, there was obviously something happening.

Jock Wallace was great for me; running up those sand dunes was torture at the time but it made us incredibly fit. We won a lot of games with late goals, and that was no fluke. We had our fitness levels checked regularly, with my lung capacity tests coming out best two years in a row. My byline-to-byline running and high-energy game needed me to be really fit, so Jock made sure I was in peak condition. It was a sad day when he left for Leicester. I have to say, though, that Willie Waddell was the biggest influence on my Rangers career. He saw that I had great drive and enthusiasm, and he turned me into that midfield player who covered every inch of the pitch, instead of the ball player that had arrived from St Johnstone. My manager there, the great Rangers goalkeeper of the 1940s and 1950s, Bobby Brown, described me as his best ever signing. That's a compliment I'll never forget.

When John took over as manager, we had some great nights in Europe, and I scored memorable headers against Juventus and PSV Eindhoven. But we didn't win the league, and by May 1980 my Rangers career was over and I moved to Hearts. I was there for ten years, a player then a manager, and I look back on my time there with great pride even though we didn't win the trophies we deserved to. One of my favourite memories was in the maroon when I scored a late goal against Rangers not long after I had moved to Edinburgh. It wasn't just the Hearts fans who cheered it, but the Rangers fans did too. They wanted to show they had appreciated my efforts in a blue jersey, and the hairs on the back of my neck still stand up when I think about it.

After more good years at Airdrie, which included two cup final appearances, I left the game I love. These days, I am a matchday hospitality host at Ibrox, which I really enjoy. The atmosphere at the new seated stadium is maybe different from when it was mainly standing, but it is every bit as good. The European nights in the last few years have been wonderful.

Jock Wallace once told us that Rangers don't play friendlies, and he was absolutely right. Wearing that jersey means winning, and winning for the supporters, your team-mates and for the manager. I like to tell people that when you include friendlies and pre-season competitions, I actually played over 550 games and scored 112 goals. I'm proud of that record, and I'm proud of my place in Rangers' history. And a great season in that history was 1977/78. I hope you enjoy reading about it.

1
Pre-Season: New Faces

AFTER THE magnificent treble success of 1975/76, Rangers looked set to dominate Scottish football with a team packed full of experienced players who had developed the winning habit. With the astute and motivational Jock Wallace at the helm, the Ibrox support enjoyed the summer of 1976 confident that the recent years of Celtic success were finally over.

But the following season was one of massive disappointment. The team slipped behind Celtic in the league race from early on, the Parkhead men no doubt boosted by the return to the dugout of Jock Stein, who had missed virtually all of the previous campaign after suffering serious injuries in a car accident in the summer of 1975. The League Cup defence ended with a humiliating 5-1 Hampden semi-final loss to Ally McLeod's Aberdeen, and in a season where several key players missed significant spells through injury, the championship challenge misfired too often with no wins in the four Old Firm meetings. Celtic ended up well clear, and then to compound the misery of all at Ibrox, they clinched the double by defeating Rangers 1-0 in a hugely controversial Scottish Cup Final when referee

Bob Valentine awarded them a penalty for handball against Derek Johnstone when it appeared to most observers that the ball had struck his knee. Seeing former hero Alfie Conn celebrate the victory in a Celtic jersey just made the day even more depressing.

There were some mitigating circumstances for such a poor season, mostly injuries at key times to important players. Derek Johnstone missed the Aberdeen semi-final loss as well as a painful Ibrox Old Firm defeat during a ten-week absence which coincided with a similar spell on the sidelines for defensive stalwart Tom Forsyth. But the team seemed to lack creative spark, relying perhaps too much on the brilliant passing and crossing of Tommy McLean. Results were hopelessly inconsistent, and with the fans starting to express some displeasure, Wallace knew his side needed an injection of fresh blood before the new season got under way.

Before the dismal defeat to Aberdeen, the League Cup campaign had featured a series of epic matches with First Division Clydebank in the quarter-final, with Rangers needing four attempts to finally knock out the Kilbowie team. The star of these encounters was Clydebank winger Davie Cooper, whose close control and dazzling skills had the international players in the Rangers defence sometimes chasing shadows. On 8 June 1977, Jock Wallace paid Clydebank £100,000 to bring the 21-year-old Cooper to Ibrox, fulfilling a boyhood ambition for the player who was brought up as a fan of the club.

'I consider Cooper to be the most exciting prospect in Scottish football,' explained Wallace when asked about such a hefty fee for a player who had never started a match in the top division. 'He has a bit to come yet, but obviously I am confident he will be a great buy for us.' The player himself simply said, 'I am thrilled at the prospect of playing for Rangers.' It was a signing that excited the support, and in years to come, many would say it represented one of the best pieces of business the club had ever carried out in the transfer market. It was the start of a legendary Rangers career.

Meanwhile, Wallace had already added another talented young player to the squad towards the end of the previous season in a far less publicised move. Club scouts had recommended midfielder Bobby Russell after watching him star for Shettleston Juniors. Russell had started out with youth club Possil YM in Glasgow before being snapped up as a 16-year-old by Sunderland, who had then released him again 14 months later after he failed to settle in the north-east of England. He found a job with a whisky company back in his home city and returned to the junior game where his ability to pick a pass and to play intelligent football quickly made him stand out from the rest.

Just after his 20th birthday, Russell was invited to play in a trial match for Rangers' reserves against Dundee United and he took full advantage of his opportunity. The slim playmaker was the best player on the pitch, and Jock Wallace signed him the next day. Like Cooper, he was a lifelong Rangers supporter, although unlike Cooper he was regarded as a signing of potential rather than a player to be given the task of returning the team to the top of Scottish football.

The pre-season fixtures would see Ibrox again host the four-club Tennent Caledonian Cup the weekend before the start of the 1977/78 Premier Division, and Wallace arranged three fixtures for the team prior to this for the players to gain match practice and sharpness after their usual gruelling fitness schedule when they had returned from the summer break. The first two were to be played in the Highlands, with Ross County and Nairn County the opposition. There would then be a midweek friendly against Dundee at Dens Park before the Ibrox crowd would get to see the players tested in the Tennent Caledonian Cup against a much higher level of opposition. The final warm-up match would see Rangers travel to Rugby Park to play Kilmarnock just two days after the Ibrox tournament.

The two-match Highland tour saw Rangers open the season on Saturday, 30 July 1977 with a straightforward 4-0 win in Dingwall, Ross County being swept aside by a strong line-up. The manager made a few changes for the second match at Nairn County just two days later, among them a first outing in the top team for Bobby Russell. The game itself was more competitive than the Saturday encounter, Nairn scoring two late goals but unable to pull back the three-goal lead that Rangers had established in the first 50 minutes. But all in attendance were talking about the elegant young unknown at the heart of the Rangers midfield, Russell having created a goal for Alex MacDonald before scoring the decisive third himself.

Russell had given Jock Wallace a pleasant problem of whether to play the inexperienced youngster once the more competitive matches started, but Wallace also had a more worrying problem when Derek Johnstone limped away from the game and was immediately ruled out of the rest of pre-season. Two days after the match gave the first sign of what Wallace thought of Russell, when the manager allowed midfielder Ian McDougall to leave the club and sign for Dundee for a fee of £15,000.

Dundee were the opposition that evening in a friendly, which was used by Wallace to give his fringe players some needed match time. Again, it seemed telling that Russell was not included in the squad, but Johnny Hamilton, a mainstay of the midfield in both previous seasons, was included in the starting 11. Most attention was on Dundee's new face, the former Celtic winger Jimmy Johnstone having signed on at Dens Park for his former team-mate Tommy Gemmell, who was the manager at the club. The match ended 1-1, with Johnstone overshadowed by the performance of teenage winger Billy MacKay for Rangers, whose pace and direct running excited the fans who had made the journey to watch the action. In contrast, Johnstone limped off after failing to impress, with it later being confirmed that he had picked up a hamstring injury and would miss the next Dundee match.

The Tennent Caledonian Cup was in its second season, played between two Scottish and two English teams, with semi-finals on day one, then a third-place match preceding the final on day two. Rangers had lost to FA Cup holders Southampton in the inaugural final in 1976, and the Saints were back to defend their trophy, alongside an exciting West Bromwich Albion side managed by Ron Atkinson and Alex Ferguson's St Mirren, who had just won Scotland's First Division and would play in the Premier Division for the first time. The opening-day fixtures saw West Brom take on St Mirren, while Rangers were given the chance to avenge their final loss when up against Southampton.

Around 40,000 attended on the Saturday and they were treated to some excellent entertainment. West Brom got the better of St Mirren in a thrilling 4-3 win, featuring a hat-trick for midfielder Tony Brown and a winning goal by future England captain Bryan Robson. Also appearing for Albion was former Rangers hero Willie Johnston, whose explosive pace and wing magic had certainly been missed by many on the terraces since his move south in 1972 not long after his double in Barcelona helped the team to European Cup Winners' Cup glory.

This was a fine West Brom team, who were seen as genuine contenders for silverware in the upcoming English season, and many onlookers were also impressed by their Paisley opponents who looked more than capable of competing in Scotland's top flight.

The team chosen by Wallace to play Southampton was without the injured pair Colin Jackson and Derek Johnstone, and it included both Russell and Cooper to give them both their Ibrox bow in the blue of Rangers. Inspirational captain John Greig filled in at centre-back beside Tom Forsyth in the absence of both his more regular partners, with Bobby McKean given the number ten shirt.

After the despair at how the previous season had ended, the fans hoped to see signs of a Rangers team back in the groove again, with Cooper being the player most eyes were on given his rising reputation within the game after his summer call-up into the Scotland national squad for the first time. He didn't disappoint, scoring a magnificent free kick to settle the match as Rangers roared to an impressive 3-1 win. Alex MacDonald had scored the first from a typical raking finish, with Derek Parlane also getting his name on the scoresheet. It wouldn't be the last free-kick goal those in blue would enjoy watching from the new number 11. With Russell looking like a seasoned veteran in the middle of the park, the new boys couldn't have wished for a better start in front of the demanding Ibrox crowd, and the fans went home happy with what they saw, confident the trophy would be won the next day.

Another 40,000 attended on the Sunday, but the weather had taken a turn for the worse overnight and the rain lashed down for much of the day. Southampton took third place in the appetiser for the day after a match that had just about everything. Referee Hugh Alexander showed a first-half red card to Southampton's John Sharp, awarded both teams a penalty, and the crowd were treated to a brilliant solo goal by Peter Osgood as the English side beat St Mirren 2-1.

The vast majority of the crowd were there for the final, of course, and Wallace named an unchanged 11 just 24 hours after that fine win over Southampton. West Brom gave Willie Johnston the captaincy for the day, but the goodwill stopped at the first whistle as the game quickly became one of sharp tackling and few chances. Davie Cooper saw a long-range shot well saved by goalkeeper Tony Godden in about the only highlight of a forgettable first 45 minutes.

Rangers were slightly the better team in a very tight affair, until referee Bill Anderson gave their opponents a helping hand to open the scoring after an hour. Peter McCloy rose to gather a corner and was clearly barged by a visiting defender as he jumped alongside. The big goalkeeper dropped the ball, and there was West Brom's highly rated attacker Laurie Cunningham to smash it home. The referee signalled a goal and was immediately surrounded by protesting Rangers players, then he was greeted to a chorus of booing from the home fans. He was unmoved, however, and from that moment on there only looked one winner.

The Midlands outfit started finding holes in the Rangers defence as the home team had to push forward in search of an equaliser, and shortly after substitute Chris Robertson missed a good chance to equalise, that man Cunningham wrapped up the match when he buried a headed knock-down in the box past McCloy. Rangers were chasing shadows towards the end, and the home fans who stayed until the final whistle were relieved the scoreline didn't get any worse than 2-0. To a mixed reception, Willie Johnston received the Tennent Caledonian Cup (after an initial mix-up when he was initially presented with the smaller trophy for third place), and the sponsors unanimously voted Laurie Cunningham the player of the tournament.

Although without a couple of important players, most in the crowd left the stadium with an uneasy feeling about the season ahead, and Jock Wallace also spoke of his disappointment after a display that saw the team well beaten. The manager also confirmed that the missing Colin Jackson may be fit enough to play some of the Rugby Park friendly the following Tuesday in the hope he would then be in contention for a place in the league opener at Pittodrie the next Saturday. With Derek Johnstone definitely out injured, plus John Greig and Tommy McLean unable to play due to suspension, it was already looking like a tough start to the new season.

Jackson successfully negotiated the Kilmarnock match, where he was mainly surrounded by fringe players and youngsters. Rangers won 3-2 with goals by Chris Robertson, Martin Henderson and young substitute Derek Strickland, who at just 17 years old was seen as a star of the future by the Ibrox coaching staff. Kilmarnock fielded a strong team, including Gordon Smith, a player manager Wallace rated highly and was watching closely. The boss didn't see his performance on the night, however, as he had jetted out to Switzerland that morning to spy on the Young Boys of Berne team who were due at Ibrox a week later in the preliminary round of the European Cup Winners' Cup.

Wallace returned, telling reporters that although he had watched Young Boys lose 4-1 to Servette, he had been impressed and they represented as tough a challenge as the FC Zürich team who had eliminated Rangers from the European Cup the previous season. The press were far more interested in a story from the other side of Glasgow, however, as Celtic confirmed their captain Kenny Dalglish

PRE-SEASON: NEW FACES

had agreed to join European champions Liverpool in a record deal for a Scottish club. This news certainly brightened the mood among the Rangers support, as without doubt the loss of their best player would weaken the Celtic assault on honours.

On Friday, 12 August, Wallace confirmed his squad of 13 players for the trip north for the league opener, to face an Aberdeen team now managed by old foe Billy McNeill. Colin Jackson was in the travelling party, and with no Greig, Johnstone or McLean to call on he also included new signing Davie Cooper, pre-season revelation Bobby Russell and young winger Billy MacKay. The build-up was now over; season 1977/78 started now.

2

August: Unrest on the Terraces

A TRIP to Aberdeen on the opening day represented a huge early test for Rangers, with the Dons' summer appointment of Clyde boss and former Celtic hero Billy McNeill adding extra spice. On a sunny day in the north-east, the Rangers fans were given the perfect opportunity to exercise their voices just before kick-off when the new Pittodrie chief walked out on to the pitch in a bright red shirt and waved to his new fans.

Needless to say, his reception from the visiting support was less than warm!

With his team selection limited by injuries and suspension, Jock Wallace was able to field an experienced defence but an untried forward line, with only one survivor in the attacking side from the cup final defeat in May.

There were senior debuts for both winger Billy MacKay and midfielder Bobby Russell, and a first top-division start for summer signing Davie Cooper. Incredibly, centre-forward Derek Parlane was the only player in the front line over the age of 21, the Scotland international being almost a veteran at the age of 24.

AUGUST: UNREST ON THE TERRACES

Aberdeen v Rangers
Saturday, 13 August 1977, Pittodrie
Peter McCloy, Sandy Jardine, Alex Miller, Tom Forsyth, Colin Jackson, Alex MacDonald, Billy MacKay, Bobby Russell, Derek Parlane, Chris Robertson, Davie Cooper
Substitutes: Johnny Hamilton, Bobby McKean

As usual on the opening day, the fans turned out in good number, with just under 22,000 in the ground to create a thunderous atmosphere. It was the home team who flew out of the traps and Joe Harper almost opened the scoring in the first two minutes when his shot flew inches wide. Davie Cooper had the first attempt on the Aberdeen goal a few minutes later, but the match was being played mainly towards Peter McCloy and the Reds grabbed a deserved lead after 11 minutes when an Ian Fleming cut-back was blasted beyond McCloy by inside-forward Drew Jarvie.

This encouraged the home support to increase the noise levels even further, the young Rangers attack rarely seen as Aberdeen continued to pour forward. But gradually, Rangers began to gain a foothold in the match, with the calm play of debutant Russell particularly impressive as he started to get more time on the ball and find team-mates with probing passes. He was involved when Derek Parlane forced the first real save from Bobby Clark on the half hour, then a couple of minutes later he went one better.

A MacKay corner was headed clear to Russell at the edge of the Aberdeen penalty area. He tried to chip a cross towards Colin Jackson but he was beaten in the air by a defender. The ball dropped 16 yards out to Cooper, who beautifully controlled it on his thigh before dinking a delightful pass into Russell's path as he raced into the box in support. The midfielder lashed an unstoppable shot high into the net past Clark before the experienced goalkeeper could narrow the angle. What a memorable moment for Russell, already looking like a player born to play on the big stage.

The goal breathed new life into Rangers, and for the first time in the match Aberdeen looked under pressure. There were no more clear chances before half-time, however, and the away fans seemed the happier at the interval considering their inexperienced line-up and the torrid opening spell they had watched.

Rangers continued to force the issue at the start of the second period, forcing a succession of corners but never troubling Clark. McCloy was forced into action after 58 minutes when he made an outstanding save from a Jarvie shot, but the Rangers defence didn't heed the warning and in the space of a couple of minutes the game looked lost. First, in an almost identical goal to their opener, Aberdeen regained the lead after 60 minutes when Jarvie again smashed home a cut-back, then less than two minutes later Harper took advantage of hesitancy in the rearguard to score the third.

The Rangers fans were stunned into silence, with the sight of a jubilant Billy McNeill on the touchline adding to their misery. Jock Wallace took off teenager MacKay and sent on the more experienced Bobby McKean to try to find a way back into proceedings, but the Aberdeen defence held firm, well marshalled by their young centre-back pairing of Willie Garner and Willie Miller. There would be no Rangers comeback, and it was McNeill who wore the widest smile in the stadium as he shook hands with Wallace after referee Tommy Muirhead brought the match to an end.

Despite the defeat, the Rangers boss was upbeat in his analysis of the game, with his young forward line given much praise. 'Players like Russell, MacKay, Robertson and

Cooper were treading new ground today,' he said, 'and they came through it well. We can go forward from here.' He also compared the debut of Russell to watching the early career of the late John White, the brilliant midfield general of the great Tottenham Hotspur team of the early 1960s. It was an amazing compliment for a player so early in his senior career, but Russell was already looking to be a sensational discovery.

As the team made their way back down to Glasgow, Wallace's thoughts were already turning towards Europe and the visit of Young Boys in just four days' time. And he wasn't finished in the transfer market as on the Monday, long-time target Gordon Smith arrived at Ibrox after Kilmarnock accepted an offer of £65,000 for the versatile attacker. On hearing this news, many Rangers fans expressed surprise as Smith had recently been playing at outside-left for the Ayrshire team, a position that Wallace had already spent big money on by securing the services of Davie Cooper. Wallace, however, had first spotted Smith when he played as an attacking inside-forward, and this was the role he had in mind for the Kilwinning-born 22-year-old. He saw the arrival of the intelligent Smith as the last piece of the jigsaw in creating a team capable of regaining the title. It was a transfer that had a lasting impact on the manager, as Wallace revealed in an interview after his career was over that he regarded Smith as his greatest signing.

Smith was a part-time player at Rugby Park, studying a business degree at the same time as forging his career on the pitch. His fitness wasn't at the same level demanded by Wallace of his players, so Smith was assured that he would be given the chance to reach full fitness before starting for the first team. That meant he would settle for a place on the bench when the Swiss came calling. Smith summed up his delight at joining his boyhood heroes when telling the press, 'It is a truly great feeling to be a Ranger. I can still hardly believe it.'

Rangers v Young Boys
Wednesday, 17 August 1977, Ibrox
Peter McCloy, Sandy Jardine, John Greig, Tom Forsyth, Colin Jackson, Alex MacDonald, Tommy McLean, Bobby Russell, Derek Parlane, Chris Robertson, Davie Cooper
Substitutes: Billy MacKay, Gordon Smith

It was no great surprise that Wallace decided to bring back his two massively experienced players who had missed the Pittodrie defeat due to suspension, with captain John Greig's leadership and winger Tommy McLean's craft both vital components of the team. Derek Johnstone was still missing through injury, although he would have been suspended anyway after being red-carded in the defeat to another Swiss outfit, FC Zürich, in the previous season. This meant young Chris Robertson would continue up front alongside Derek Parlane and be expected to find the goals that the usually prolific Johnstone could be relied upon to provide.

A good crowd of around 30,000 were inside Ibrox to see what they hoped was the start of a better European campaign than the fans had endured in recent seasons, but if they were hoping to see an entertaining match it soon became apparent the visitors had no intention of providing excitement. From the first minute Young Boys employed ultra-negative tactics, with their packed defence frequently sending back-passes to their goalkeeper Gérard Weissbaum, and a well-practised offside trap often foiling the Rangers attack. The sudden passing of music legend Elvis Presley the previous evening was providing as much conversation for the fans as the football they were watching.

Rangers struggled to gain any fluency as the match was littered with stoppages. A Colin Jackson header that narrowly missed the target was the only brief moment of goal threat in a turgid opening half hour, and as the interval started to approach, so did the unrest on the terraces. Then on 39 minutes, the man who Rangers so often turned to in their hour of need again came up with inspiration. A Tom Forsyth through ball signalled another moment for the Young Boys defence to step forward in unison to play the attackers offside, but they had failed to notice Greig's perfectly timed forward run from deep. As the Swiss defence desperately chased back, the skipper composed himself before smashing his shot into the net off a post.

With the half-time score at 1-0, the fans wondered if Young Boys would now be more positive in the second period. But their German manager Kurt Linder seemed perfectly content with a single-goal deficit, and the match continued in the same pattern as before. It was the other full-back, Sandy Jardine, who came closest to adding to the lead, when his ferocious shot cannoned off the woodwork with Weissbaum well beaten.

As the half wore on, Wallace threw on both his substitutes to see if they could unlock the packed defence, with new signing Gordon Smith getting a warm ovation on his Ibrox debut. But there would be no further goals, the match ending with Jackson firing tamely into the side-netting in injury time when in a great position. It had been a hugely frustrating night, summed up by Wallace when he said, 'I am disappointed, but we are ahead. We will obviously have to play a different game in Berne.' Meanwhile, a relieved Linder told the press, 'We were a little bit lucky to lose only one goal. Rangers can play much better, and Johnstone will be back. We are not through to the next round yet.'

After the dismal end to the previous season, then the West Bromwich Albion and Aberdeen defeats, the match had done little to alter the negative mood among many of the Ibrox regulars. The pre-season optimism had already been replaced by a feeling that the team had to improve quickly, and that had to start the following Saturday when Hibs were the first visitors of the season to Ibrox on league business. They would need to defeat their Edinburgh rivals without their skipper, as Greig still had the remainder of his domestic suspension to serve. There would be no first-team return for Derek Johnstone, either, but he was selected for the reserve team with the hope he could show he was ready for the European match to come.

Rangers v Hibernian
Saturday, 20 August 1977, Ibrox
Peter McCloy, Sandy Jardine, Alex Miller, Tom Forsyth, Colin Jackson, Alex MacDonald, Tommy McLean, Bobby Russell, Derek Parlane, Chris Robertson, Davie Cooper
Substitutes: Billy MacKay, Gordon Smith.

It was a slight surprise that Wallace went with ten of the same players against Hibs, the only change being the enforced return of Alex Miller. The team had struggled in attack, and with Martin Henderson and the veteran Colin Stein playing in the reserves, many felt that one of them would replace young Chris Robertson who had rarely looked like scoring so far. Gordon Smith had enjoyed a promising debut in midweek but he was left on the bench again. Few in the 23,000 crowd seemed to be in agreement with the manager's team selection when it became known, so it was important the 11 started well and silenced the doubters. They did the opposite.

There were only four minutes on the clock when Hibs midfielder Bobby Smith let fly for goal, Peter McCloy making the save but only able to parry the ball back out into the penalty area. The entire Rangers backline stood still, allowing youngster Gordon Rae to latch on to the rebound and thump it into the net with McCloy still on the ground. It was a terrible goal to lose, and even though there was almost an entire 90 minutes left to play, there seemed an inevitability about it being a defining moment.

For the remainder of the first half Rangers toiled badly, just as in midweek struggling to break down a well-drilled defence. Tom Forsyth was about the only Rangers player who could be exempted from criticism as he snuffed out several Hibs counterattacks as well as trying to push forward if the opportunity arose. Robertson and Derek Parlane were dejected-looking figures, their markers barely giving them an inch of space, and the ball rarely being played into an area they could attack. The half-time whistle was met by loud booing, with the occasional chant of 'What a load of rubbish' heard from the home support.

Wallace chose to allow the same 11 players to start the second half, and they continued to huff and puff without seriously threatening Mike McDonald in the visiting goal. Smith replaced Davie Cooper midway through the half but this did nothing to liven up the attack in a season that no forward had yet scored in. With the minutes ticking away, the howls of frustration from the fans started to turn into anger with chants of 'Wallace must go' now being sung. In the closing stages, as Rangers threw men forward vainly searching for a face-saving equaliser, Hibs mounted a swift counter, which ended in Ally McLeod releasing midfield man Des Bremner clean through on McCloy. His impudent chip over the goalkeeper and into the net was the signal for a mass walkout by the fans, and the demand for the manager's removal spreading throughout the ground.

Typically, Wallace refused to hide away from the media after this painful 2-0 loss, and answered questions on whether his future was now in doubt. 'The fans pay their money, and if they are not satisfied with what they see, then they are entitled to show their displeasure,' was how he answered journalists. He also brushed off the idea of resigning, and confirmed that Derek Johnstone was in contention to return to the team in midweek, when the League Cup campaign was to start with a home second round first leg tie against St Johnstone of the First Division. A poor result in that match might mean the question would be asked again.

Aberdeen were the early league leaders after two wins from two games, with Rangers rooted at the bottom with no points. Defending champions Celtic weren't much higher, as they had lost to Ayr United and only had one point from their opening matches. Some newspapers spoke of this potentially being the season when there might finally be an end to the Old Firm stranglehold on the title, with Kilmarnock in 1965 the last team outside the big two to be champions.

Wallace was in typically bullish mood at the pre-League Cup press conference, where 24 hours before the match he announced his starting 11. Unsurprisingly, he made several changes, four in total. He confirmed that Johnstone was back to lead the forward line, despite speculation during the summer that his future at the club would be back in the centre-half role in which he also excelled. Also returning from injury was midfielder Kenny Watson, and he would start alongside teenage winger Billy MacKay. Experienced heads Tommy McLean, Derek Parlane and Alex MacDonald were out, as was young striker Robertson to allow a first start for Smith. The manager asked the fans to be patient with a team containing so many inexperienced players, saying that if they were to boo anyone it should be him; the players needed encouragement.

Rangers v St Johnstone
Wednesday, 24 August 1977, Ibrox
Peter McCloy, Sandy Jardine, Alex Miller, Tom Forsyth, Colin Jackson, Kenny Watson, Billy MacKay, Bobby Russell, Derek Johnstone, Gordon Smith, Davie Cooper
Substitutes: Tommy McLean, Chris Robertson

St Johnstone looked to be awkward opponents having won both of their opening First Division matches without conceding a goal. Rangers took to the field in their change strip of white shirts and blue shorts, with the crowd of only 10,000 a sign of the displeasure among the fans at how the season had started. The attendance wasn't helped by monsoon-like rain falling on Glasgow during the evening, many deciding that staying warm indoors was a better option.

The combination of a small crowd and the recent results combined to give the old stadium an eerily quiet atmosphere as the game started, and it stayed that way in the early stages as Rangers struggled to find the goal they needed to get the support back onside. After half an hour of goalless action, with Bobby Russell again standing out in midfield, St Johnstone scored with virtually their first meaningful attack. It was a disaster for the usually dependable Tom Forsyth, as the Scotland centre-back misjudged a long high ball and only succeeded in heading it straight to Perth forward John Brogan. He quickly and efficiently despatched it behind Peter McCloy to give the underdogs the lead, and to restart the rumblings of discontent in the home support.

If the scoreline had stayed this way for any length of time then things may have turned ugly again for the manager. But five minutes before the break, Johnstone reminded everyone what Rangers had been missing. A beautifully flighted Cooper corner was met by the head of Johnstone at the back post, and goalkeeper Derek Robertson was well beaten. It was an equaliser that came along at exactly the right time, and it gave the home team the belief they had been lacking.

Johnstone was again at the heart of the action when Rangers took the lead just ten minutes into the second half. He collected the ball inside the Saints penalty box, and was brought crashing to the floor by a reckless John O'Brien tackle. Referee Mike Delaney could only make one decision, and it was 2-1 when Alex Miller scored easily from the spot. With a second leg to come at Muirton Park, a single-goal lead represented a potentially tricky return leg, but any nerves were eased with a third goal after 71 minutes. Again it was created by Cooper, his clever cross again finding Johnstone, who swept the ball into the net for his second goal of the game.

The match ended 3-1 but the St Johnstone players left the field still furious at Delaney who decided against awarding them a last-minute penalty when the ball looked to have struck Colin Jackson's hand. Overall it was a patchy performance, but with two assists for Cooper, another polished display by Russell, and a promising first 90 minutes for Smith, the new-look Rangers promised better days ahead. Wallace summed things up by saying, 'There was plenty to like in the way we played. It was far from perfect, but it is up to us to take it from here.'

Firhill was the venue for the weekend league fixture, with Wallace suggesting that his team selection would have the return European match in Berne in mind. Many assumed this suggested a return for the more seasoned players who had dropped out for the League Cup tie, a tough away fixture on the continent probably not the ideal place to play so many inexperienced players. Partick Thistle had beaten Rangers the last time the teams had met at Firhill, and with former Celtic star Bertie Auld in charge, they represented a difficult hurdle to the Ibrox side securing their first league win.

Partick Thistle v Rangers
Saturday 27 August 1977, Firhill
Peter McCloy, Sandy Jardine, Alex Miller, Tom Forsyth, Colin Jackson, Alex MacDonald, Tommy McLean, Bobby Russell, Derek Johnstone, Gordon Smith, Davie Cooper
Substitutes: Derek Parlane, Kenny Watson

Apart from the still-suspended John Greig, this looked as close to Rangers' strongest 11 as had played all season. The big crowd of over 18,500 got to see the best performance of the campaign so far. The first half was mainly played towards Thistle goalkeeper Alan Rough, who showed his international ability several times. The home team did threaten occasionally, but they would have been happy to get to half-time level. They got within 30 seconds of achieving that only for a moment of controversy as the crowd were starting to think of an interval pie.

Smith went down in the penalty area under a heavy challenge by new signing Ronnie Sheed, referee Ian Foote immediately awarding the penalty. The Thistle players disagreed furiously as did Auld on the sidelines, but Alex Miller ignored the furore and calmly slotted the ball home from 12 yards. The half-time whistle sounded seconds after Partick had kicked off again, the perfect end to the half for Rangers. They then took full advantage of their lead in the second half as they produced their finest 45 minutes for some time.

If not for Rough in goal, the match would have been over within a few minutes of the restart, but the incessant pressure on the home defence told in the 54th minute when Smith marked his first league start with his first goal for the club, a header from eight yards out. The Rangers fans who had so vocally criticised the players and manager just seven days earlier were now in full voice and enjoying what they saw. Somehow the Firhill side kept the score the same until the last ten minutes when a brilliant Bobby Russell shot and a second goal for Smith gave the final score of 4-0 a more realistic look.

With Aberdeen dropping their first points in a draw with Dundee United, and Celtic slumping to another defeat at home to Motherwell, all of a sudden the Rangers fans could look at the league table again. They were still in a lowly seventh place but at last heading in the right direction. When asked after the game if he would adopt a more defensive approach in Berne, Wallace growled, 'Defend? You have to be joking! We have a side geared to attack, we go to Berne to increase our lead, not defend it.' Confidence was returning to Ibrox and the month of August in domestic football was ending much more positively than it had begun.

When Rangers arrived in Switzerland, Wallace confirmed that captain Greig would come back into the team, his domestic suspension not in effect when playing in European competition. Young Boys had been enduring an even worse start to their season than Rangers, still looking for a first win in the league after four matches. The Wankdorf Stadium in Berne saw a crowd of 21,000 for the visit of the Scots, with Rangers only making that one change from the team who had impressed at Firhill four days earlier.

Young Boys v Rangers
Wednesday 31 August 1977, Wankdorf Stadium
Peter McCloy, Sandy Jardine, John Greig, Tom Forsyth, Colin Jackson, Alex MacDonald, Tommy McLean, Bobby Russell, Derek Johnstone, Gordon Smith, Davie Cooper
Substitutes: Alex Miller, Bobby McKean

For a team who needed to win to progress, Young Boys were surprisingly negative in the opening stages, perhaps fearing the away goal that could make their task all the more difficult. Rangers settled into the game the better despite an early injury to Tommy McLean that saw substitute Bobby McKean enter before 20 minutes had passed. The Swiss looked like a team near the foot of their league table, short of confidence and devoid of attacking intent.

With Bobby Russell and Alex MacDonald in charge of the midfield, it was Rangers who always looked the team more likely to break the deadlock and they thought they had found that vital opener in the 40th minute only to see the Italian referee disallow MacDonald's effort. But just three minutes later it was 1-0 to the visitors. It was already a familiar strike, a Davie Cooper corner met by a towering Derek Johnstone header, and the ball was in the net past a different Swiss goalkeeper in Walter Eichenberger. The

Rangers bench celebrated, knowing Young Boys now needed three goals to progress. Surely an impossible task for a team that had shown so little in attack.

Rangers started the second half in confident mood, and their small travelling support were in good voice. But things started to change just three minutes after kick-off. A snap shot by forward Josef Küttel had Peter McCloy beaten but crashed off the post. The retreating Colin Jackson tried to clear the rebound for a corner but miscued and sliced the ball into his own net for a bizarre and undeserved equaliser on the night. Suddenly, the home team were energised, and they flooded forward. Wallace responded by withdrawing young Russell and bringing on the experienced defender Alex Miller, pushing Greig into a more midfield role.

But Young Boys weren't to be denied, and in an increasingly frenzied atmosphere they scored again on the hour. There was some controversy over the goal, with Derek Johnstone lying on the turf for almost a minute after a clash with a Swiss defender, the referee refusing to stop play to allow treatment. With Rangers temporarily a man short, the ball fell to substitute Jost Leuzinger after an initial shot had again hit the post, and he smashed the ball into the net. Angry Rangers players surrounded the referee, but Riccardo Lattanzi of Italy waved them away and Wallace's men were suddenly within a goal of elimination.

Wallace often spoke of the need for players at the club to possess character, a determination and will to succeed no matter the circumstances. In the next 15 minutes he was to see his side display his favourite attribute. Rangers, fuelled by a sense of injustice, reimposed themselves on the match, and started pushing their hosts back again as the crowd roared on their opponents while sensing the possibility of a huge upset. Their hopes were extinguished with 19 minutes left when Rangers grabbed the goal that killed the tie. A superb through pass by substitute Bobby McKean found Smith bursting beyond the home defence, and the former Kilmarnock man further endeared himself to his new fans by confidently drilling the ball home.

Young Boys now needed two goals again, and with time running out and a determined Rangers standing in their way, it never looked like happening. But there was one last controversial moment to come, one that had consequences for the next round. Johnstone had been subjected to some rough tactics all evening, the Swiss defence aware of the danger he represented. For the umpteenth time he was clattered by a centre-half, and the big striker's temper snapped as he lashed out in retaliation. The referee immediately produced the red card; incredibly Johnstone had now been sent off twice in Switzerland in the space of a year, the only two red cards of his Ibrox career.

It was a bitter end to a pulsating match and Wallace was still furious when speaking to the press afterwards. It meant another European suspension for Johnstone, who would miss at least the first leg of the first round tie against the Dutchmen of FC Twente. Wallace barked, 'I am very angry at the sending off of Johnstone. We have to live with it, it has happened and we can't change anything.' The boss also found time to praise his team, both for their polished display before half-time and then their grit and determination after going behind.

August was now over with Rangers now looking to be on the up after their terrible start. The new signings were all playing their part, the team were now scoring goals, and so there was optimism that September would see things continue to improve. It looked a pivotal month, with the first Old Firm clash of the season looming on 10 September. But Rangers had to complete their League Cup tie with St Johnstone in Perth before thoughts could turn to the biggest match of the season so far.

3

September: The Comeback

THE LEAGUE Cup first round second leg away to St Johnstone seemed to be the first match of the new season where Rangers weren't under any pressure prior to kick-off. With a 3-1 lead against lower-league opposition, and a team that had found goalscoring form, there was a relaxed air among the supporters who travelled to Muirton Park in a crowd of 11,000. Jock Wallace's men had suffered a few injuries in the midweek tussle in Berne, and with skipper John Greig serving the last match of his domestic suspension for a dismissal in the last league game of 1976/77 at Pittodrie, it seemed a good time to freshen the team up slightly and give a couple of players with less recent game time some minutes on the pitch.

St Johnstone v Rangers
Saturday, 3 September 1977, Muirton Park
Peter McCloy, Sandy Jardine, Alex Miller, Derek Johnstone, Colin Jackson, Alex MacDonald, Bobby McKean, Bobby Russell, Derek Parlane, Gordon Smith, Davie Cooper
Substitutes: Kenny Watson, Martin Henderson

With Tom Forsyth ruled out, Derek Johnstone was given the chance to show his versatility by slotting into the centre-back role in which he was also a Scotland international. Tommy McLean hadn't recovered from his injury in Berne, allowing midweek replacement Bobby McKean to start on the right wing. Bobby Russell was declared fit after taking a knock in Berne and being substituted. Wallace was flying out to Holland after the match to spy on Rangers' upcoming European opponents, and maybe he told the team he wanted to get away early as they roared out the blocks and had the match finished in the opening 20 minutes.

Derek Parlane hadn't managed to get on the scoresheet in his earlier starts before losing his place to Derek Johnstone, but it took him only a quarter of an hour to show he still knew the way to goal when he found space in the Saints' penalty area to grab the opener. And as the Perth men tried to recover from this setback, referee Mike Delaney awarded Rangers a penalty just moments later when McKean was felled. Alex Miller beat goalkeeper Derek Robertson from 12 yards and already thoughts were turning to the massive match the following weekend.

Johnstone strolled through the game, looking the best player on the pitch despite this being his first start in defence for some time. Wallace had a big decision to make for the Old Firm match if Forsyth didn't make it, as Johnstone was his first-choice centre-forward.

After that early blitz, Rangers seemed content with playing possession football and the match reached half-time with the score unchanged at 2-0. The second half was also something of a stroll, both Kenny Watson and Martin Henderson coming on as the First Division outfit struggled to lay a glove on vastly superior opponents. It looked like they might escape with just a two-goal defeat, until the

83rd minute when a slightly more realistic look was given to the scoreline as Gordon Smith added to his impressive early goal return for the club when he headed in a cross from Johnstone.

What had been a close to perfect day was marred right at the end when man of the match Johnstone limped off after a heavy tackle. The Rangers fans still in the ground held their breath, hoping their star man would be fit and available for the Ibrox visit of Celtic in seven days' time.

On his return from his Dutch spying mission, Wallace was greeted with the news that UEFA had called a disciplinary session which would discuss the length of ban for Johnstone, meaning he would almost certainly sit out both legs against Twente. The Dutch had impressed him in their 3-1 league win over Go Ahead Eagles, and he expressed the view that they were a much superior team to Young Boys and his players would need to be at their best to get through the tie. Meanwhile, the preparations for the weekend Old Firm clash saw Celtic make a double signing with the arrivals of Tom McAdam from Dundee United and John Dowie from Fulham. Both managers had to sweat on key players coming through midweek international fixtures, with Celtic captain Danny McGrain playing for Scotland in East Germany while Davie Cooper, Kenny Watson and Celtic's Tommy Burns were in the under-21 side that faced Switzerland at Ibrox. Forsyth and Johnstone had been named to travel to Berlin but both were withdrawn through injury.

Rangers also found out their opponents in the third round of the League Cup, and no doubt it was the tie of the round. Cup holders and league leaders Aberdeen were to stand between Rangers and the quarter-finals, with the first leg at Ibrox on Wednesday, 5 October.

All those on international duty came through the matches unscathed, with Cooper shining for the young Scots as he scored a goal and assisted another in a 3-1 win. Attention could now turn to the biggest club game of all, with Ibrox the venue for the season's first clash of the giants of Scottish football. Wallace was able to pick from a bigger squad than he had at one time feared, with both Forsyth and Johnstone declared fit plus the return of John Greig after his marathon suspension. Meanwhile, at Parkhead, Jock Stein was still looking for the right blend after losing Kenny Dalglish on the eve of the season, and he was still without former Ranger Alfie Conn who suffered a knee injury on the opening day.

With both clubs suffering poor starts in the league, there was a strange look about an Old Firm match where the combatants were in the bottom half of the table. Defeat for Celtic would mean their worst start to a campaign in memory, as they had just one point from their opening three fixtures. With their midweek signings both set to be given their debuts, and with Rangers also fielding their three recent recruits, the scene was set for the next chapter of this great rivalry. And what a feast the teams provided for the 51,000 fans inside the stadium.

Rangers v Celtic
Saturday, 10 September 1977, Ibrox
Peter McCloy, Sandy Jardine, Alex Miller, Tom Forsyth, Derek Johnstone, Alex MacDonald, Bobby McKean, Bobby Russell, Derek Parlane, Gordon Smith, Davie Cooper
Substitutes: John Greig, Tommy McLean

There were a few surprises in the Rangers team selection. Wallace decided not to bring back Greig due to his limited match time so far, the skipper making his first domestic appearance of the season on the bench. He also kept faith with Bobby McKean, who had played so well in Berne and Perth after replacing the injured Tommy McLean, meaning the fit-again McLean was also named as a substitute. But the biggest surprise was his decision to leave Johnstone in defence and pair him with Forsyth, meaning no room in the 13 for Colin Jackson. Derek Parlane was at centre-forward as those who played well in Perth were rewarded.

It was something of a strange occasion, an Old Firm game without any television cameras present due to a dispute at the time between the league and the TV companies. It meant the only way to see the action was to be inside the stadium, and the teams came out to a raucous welcome from their devotees. Jock Stein decided not to start both of his midweek signings, Tom McAdam watching the opening exchanges from the Celtic bench. Fellow new boy John Dowie and defender Jim Casey were the only two who started for Celtic having never played in the fixture before.

It was a typical blood-and-thunder opening, and in only the second minute Parlane suffered a nasty-looking head injury in a collision with a Celtic player. Wallace had a long discussion with the player on the touchline, along with physio Tommy Craig, and he still looked very shaken once they had agreed he was able to play on. Both teams created chances in an even opening 15 minutes, Rangers coming closest when superb crosses by Sandy Jardine and then Davie Cooper just eluded the inrushing forwards with goalkeeper Peter Latchford beaten. Celtic's best effort was a Jóhannes Eðvaldsson header that went inches over the crossbar from a John Doyle corner.

Then in the 18th minute, Eðvaldsson did find the target. A poor clearance by the Rangers defence went straight to midfielder Tommy Burns. He played a pass to Paul Wilson and ran on for the return. Burns then sent in a teasing cross that was met first time by Eðvaldsson, and the Icelander leapt into the air in celebration as his shot whistled past Peter McCloy to put Celtic a goal ahead. Rangers tried to rally immediately, and came close when Gordon Smith's 20-yard effort flew just past the post.

With Parlane still looking in some discomfort up front, Rangers were relying mostly on Smith and Cooper to threaten an equaliser, Cooper being next to cause havoc in the Celtic penalty area when his wicked cross was turned inches past his own post by centre-back Roddie MacDonald. The Rangers fans had found their voices again after the early setback, but they were stunned into silence in the 31st minute when Celtic made it 2-0. Burns was the creator once more, his cross again finding the unmarked Eðvaldsson who headed beyond McCloy for his second goal of the afternoon.

Rangers were now rattled, and when referee Ian Foote blew his whistle for half-time it looked like a second home defeat of the season was inevitable. When the team returned to the dressing room the full extent of Parlane's injury became apparent – he had suffered a broken cheekbone and had to be taken off. This meant Greig led the team out of the tunnel for the second half, and he would play in central defence with Johnstone pushed up front in Parlane's place. It was a change that dramatically paid off.

Rangers went forward from the first whistle in the second period, Johnstone now giving the team the focal point that had been missing in the first half. It took just eight minutes for the pressure to pay off. A flowing move involving Greig, Russell and Cooper ended with the ball at the feet of Johnstone inside the Celtic penalty area. His clever pass inside found the forward run of Smith, and the

SEPTEMBER: THE COMEBACK

Old Firm debutant smashed the ball past Latchford to give the Rangers supporters hope.

Rangers were now relentless, and Stein tried to stem the tide by pulling goalscorer Eðvaldsson back into defence to mark Johnstone. Goalkeeper Latchford then made two stunning saves in the space of a couple of minutes, both times denying Cooper's left-footed strikes. The Celtic penalty area was now under siege and there were still 25 minutes left to play when they conceded again. It was another great team goal, this time McKean starting the move that freed Cooper down the left, the winger slipping a perfectly weighted pass inside to Johnstone and the big striker buried his shot past Latchford.

Ibrox was now in a frenzy, the home fans roaring their approval. With Tommy McLean now on the field in place of the injured Alex MacDonald, Rangers were in total command. Latchford was Celtic's hero as he continued to make important saves, with the scores remaining level as the match entered the last ten minutes. Then, just as the visiting fans were thinking they might escape with a point, their goalkeeper made his first mistake of the day. Russell's high cross looked an easy catch for Latchford, but under no real pressure he allowed the ball to squirm from his grasp. As it dropped from his hands there was Smith, almost on the goal line, to gratefully knock the ball into the empty net and make it 3-2. The comeback was complete, with the players and supporters celebrating wildly.

Stein then threw on both his substitutes as a last throw of the dice, but Rangers were in no mood to surrender their lead, comfortably negotiating the last few minutes. Smith was the hero of the day with his double meaning he had now scored six times in just four matches. He was part of a Rangers team that had gelled, the early season stumbles now forgotten as the fans grew in confidence that they had a side destined for title glory. FC Twente coach Spitz Kohn had watched the match, and he told reporters how impressed he was with Rangers, and expressed some relief that his team would not be facing Johnstone in the first leg of their Cup Winners' Cup tie.

Wallace didn't need to go looking for problems when trying to pick a team to defeat the very useful Dutch side. As well as the suspension of Johnstone, he was now without both Parlane and Alex MacDonald after their Old Firm match injuries, and he was also concerned that Greig hadn't achieved match fitness yet after his stop-start beginning to the season. He decided to recall Kenny Watson into the midfield in place of MacDonald, with Martin Henderson given a rare opportunity to lead the forward line.

Rangers v FC Twente
Wednesday, 14 September 1977, Ibrox
Peter McCloy, Sandy Jardine, Alex Miller, Tom Forsyth, Colin Jackson, Kenny Watson, Bobby McKean, Bobby Russell, Martin Henderson, Gordon Smith, Davie Cooper
Substitutes: John Greig, Tommy McLean

After the heroics against Celtic, a decent crowd of 33,000 flocked to the stadium hoping to see a continuation of the second-half form. But the Dutch team were well organised and had a few very capable players, and they had no intention of letting the Scots take control of the match. They lined up with veteran Epi Drost playing as a sweeper behind their back four, and with former Ajax midfielder Arnold Muhren their playmaker. Both men put on a masterclass in possession football, with the initially noisy crowd soon subdued as they watched every Rangers attack break down before goalkeeper André van Gerven was needed.

It was Drost who came closest to scoring in the first half, his thundering 25-yard free kick smashing off the post with McCloy looking beaten. Rangers enjoyed much of the ball but despite some clever play from Russell and McKean, the final ball always seemed to elude a blue jersey, with it often being the excellent Drost who found himself in the right place to mop up the danger. By half-time a goal was already looking unlikely, but to Rangers' credit they refused to resort to long-ball tactics and kept trying to pass their way to success.

The second half saw much the same pattern, although the home team did start to exert more pressure on the Dutch back line. There was a series of corners which helped ramp up the noise again inside Ibrox, but none of them led to the breakthrough. Twente showed their menace on the hour when Jaap Bos found space inside the penalty area only to see McCloy save his effort, the Dutchman then hitting the rebound wide.

Halfway through the second period came the big chance the crowd had waited for. Sandy Jardine raced down the flank, and cut the ball back from the goal line into the path of Cooper who was only eight yards out. With the goal looking to be at his mercy, the winger tried to place the ball into the far corner but looked on in horror as his effort crept inches wide.

It was a massive escape for Twente, and they then retreated even further into their shell in order to avoid risking a repeat. With no Johnstone or Parlane to lead the line, Rangers looked toothless up front, and the fans had accepted the 0-0 result well before the West German referee ended the contest. Twente coach Kohn greeted his players on the touchline as they left the pitch, looking like a man whose gameplan had been executed perfectly, and looking also like a man confident of victory in the return leg. Wallace tried to be upbeat in the post-match analysis, saying his team had played a typically patient European tie, and that they had shown already they could score goals away from home in the competition. While this was true, most observers now rated FC Twente as clear favourites to progress.

Attention then turned back to the domestic challenge, and the weekend trip to Paisley to play the young and exciting St Mirren team created by manager Alex Ferguson. Saints had enjoyed a solid start to their first season back in the top flight, and sat behind leaders Aberdeen in third place, a point above Rangers. With Johnstone available again, he was always going to return to the team, and the manager also decided it was time to fit his captain back into the starting 11. Alex MacDonald was still missing with the hamstring injury picked up in the Old Firm victory, however, allowing Kenny Watson to retain his place in a much-anticipated clash that had seen all 26,000 tickets sold.

St Mirren v Rangers
Saturday, 17 September 1977, Love Street
Peter McCloy, Sandy Jardine, John Greig, Tom Forsyth, Colin Jackson, Kenny Watson, Bobby McKean, Bobby Russell, Derek Johnstone, Gordon Smith, Davie Cooper
Substitutes: Alex Miller, Martin Henderson

The atmosphere inside a packed Love Street was more like a cup tie than a routine league fixture when referee Bill Mullan started the match. And both sides seem to treat it like a cup encounter in the early stages, with full-blooded challenges and no quarter given. The young Saints team, featuring players such as Frank McGarvey, Tony Fitzpatrick

SEPTEMBER: THE COMEBACK

and Billy Stark, were showing little respect for their more famous visitors, and McCloy was the slightly busier of the goalkeepers during the first 20 minutes.

Rangers looked like they needed a goal to subdue the enthusiasm of the home team, and it was one of their experienced stars who found the moment of inspiration they were needing after 26 minutes. Bobby McKean started the move by cutting infield and running at the St Mirren defence. His cross was headed out but only to the feet of Cooper. The winger slipped a neat ball to Smith on the overlap, the former Kilmarnock man reaching the goal line before flighting over his cross. The ball was slightly behind the inrushing Jardine, but the Scotland full-back showed great technique to twist his body to fire in a volley that eluded the diving Saints goalkeeper Donald Hunter and hit the corner of the net.

It was Jardine's first goal of the season, and the massive travelling support now thought they could relax. How wrong they were. Ferguson's team came roaring back at Rangers, determined to get back into the match, and urged on by a frenzied support they took just seven minutes to equalise. Frank McGarvey got to a through ball wide on the right in front of Greig, and his low cross was thumped beyond McCloy by Brian Docherty. Rangers were now on the back foot as the eager and energetic Paisley team scented blood. Jock Wallace would have been more than happy to see his team leave the pitch at the interval still level, but with just four minutes of the half remaining Mullan awarded St Mirren a penalty for Colin Jackson's foul on Derek Hyslop. Centreforward McGarvey thumped the ball into the net, and the home fans cheered their heroes from the field with a 2-1 lead.

If Rangers didn't have enough to worry about with the events on the park, at half-time they also had to be concerned at trouble on the terraces. Fans in the away section spilled out on to the pitch to get away from bottles being thrown by their own supporters, police struggling to restore order for several minutes as missiles rained down on them. The restart was delayed for around ten minutes, and police confirmed later that 44 arrests had been made.

If the atmosphere had been fiery in the first half, it had ramped up even further now with the occasional skirmish among supporters still breaking out after the teams reappeared. The players seemed to also get caught up in the gladiatorial occasion, Tom Forsyth and Frank McGarvey having a shoving match after Rangers were awarded a free kick which resulted in a booking for Forsyth. Shortly afterwards, a linesman called over Mullan to inform him of another altercation between the players off the ball, this time leading to a red card being shown to Forsyth. Rangers were now a goal and a man down and were staring at a third league defeat of the season already.

The linesman who had been the villain of the piece to the Rangers support then redeemed himself in their eyes just before the hour when he flagged McGarvey offside as he ran through and put the ball in the net. It looked a very tight decision, television pictures the next day suggesting that the St Mirren man had scored a legitimate goal. Incredibly, while the St Mirren fans and players were still venting their anger at not being 3-1 ahead, the ten men of Rangers suddenly struck to make it 2-2. It was a first competitive goal in Rangers colours for summer signing Cooper.

Johnstone headed on a through ball and it was then won in the air again, this time by Smith. His flick on found Cooper unmarked inside the Saints' penalty box, and he lashed the ball high into the net from 12 yards with his left foot. It was the pivotal moment of the match, Rangers suddenly finding themselves all square after seeming to go two behind. This gave Rangers heart and despite having a player less they then went for a winner. Just eight more minutes had passed when the away end erupted again. Rangers won a free kick out on the right touchline, the ball being flighted in by Cooper's deadly accurate left foot. As former Rangers goalkeeper Donald Hunter hesitated, there was Johnstone rising to head the ball past him from just four yards.

Another September comeback looked complete but there was a final twist still to come. With 15 minutes left McGarvey looped a header towards goal from fully 15 yards. McCloy seemed to think it was sailing over the crossbar, but he looked on in horror as the ball went over his head then dropped under the bar and into his net. The big goalkeeper was badly at fault – and he knew it. It was a mistake that would make sure the points were shared, with both managers afterwards claiming they had done enough to win. Ferguson bemoaned both the extended half-time break and the disallowed goal as valid reasons for saying his team were unlucky overall, with Wallace unsurprisingly taking the view that the harsh dismissal of Forsyth had been a big influence on the eventual outcome. With Aberdeen defeating Celtic at Pittodrie, the men from the north moved a further point ahead at the top.

Colin Jackson was booked in the match, and this meant that he had already earned himself an appointment with the SFA disciplinary committee, who would also deal with his centre-back partner after his sending off. And to add further to future selection problems, Rangers were finally informed on the Monday morning that UEFA had imposed a three-game ban on Derek Johnstone for his red card against Young Boys, meaning he missed not only the return match against FC Twente, but the first leg of the next round should Rangers get there. With John Greig limping off at Paisley at the weekend to be replaced by Alex Miller, it all looked like there could be a defensive headache for the manager on the horizon.

Rangers had a rare midweek off but it wasn't a relaxing time for Forsyth, Jardine or Johnstone as they all were with the Scotland squad for the huge World Cup qualifier against Czechoslovakia at Hampden. Johnstone was named a substitute with the two defenders both starters, and the pair had solid games as Scotland beat the reigning European champions 3-1 to get within one match of a trip to Argentina the following summer. Cooper was also on international duty, starring in a 2-1 win for the under-21s at Tynecastle against the young Czechs.

When the international players returned to Ibrox after their exertions, Forsyth was informed by his manager that he would not be fined by the club for his sending off at Paisley, as usually happened to any player who received a red card. Wallace explained to Forsyth, and the press, that he had visited the STV studios to watch for himself the footage of the incident and had decided that a fine was not warranted. The obvious inference was that the officials had got this one wrong and the player was the victim of an injustice. He also confirmed that Greig would play no part in the weekend match as he hadn't recovered from injury, but Alex MacDonald was now fully fit and would start the match against Ayr United at Ibrox. The main headline, however, from his press conference was the decision to drop McCloy and bring back experienced backup goalkeeper Stewart Kennedy for the visit of the Honest Men. The blunder that allowed St Mirren to equalise had cost McCloy his position in the team.

SEPTEMBER: THE COMEBACK

Rangers v Ayr United
Saturday, 24 September 1977, Ibrox
Stewart Kennedy, Sandy Jardine, Alex Miller, Tom Forsyth, Colin Jackson, Alex MacDonald, Bobby McKean, Bobby Russell, Derek Johnstone, Gordon Smith, Davie Cooper
Substitutes: Tommy McLean, Iain Munro

The crowd of 20,000 arrived at Ibrox expecting a routine victory as Ayr were struggling near the foot of the table. Alex Stuart's men were tough opposition on their day, however, as they had shown earlier in the season when they defeated Celtic at Somerset Park.

The visitors employed a five-man defence in front of former Aberdeen goalkeeper Andy Geoghegan, an injury crisis forcing Stuart into playing a containing game. This allowed Rangers plenty of possession, and the first half quickly became something of a siege, Bobby Russell particularly impressive as the Ayr defence were kept busy. There had been several near misses before the inevitable happened, and it was that man Gordon Smith who again provided the breakthrough when his well-directed header gave Geoghegan no chance.

As well as Russell, centre-back Forsyth had the crowd singing his praises as he quickly snuffed out any brief danger when the Ayrshire side tried to get forward. Cooper, Johnstone and Smith all passed up presentable chances, with the visitors relieved to be only one goal down when referee Eddie Thomson ended the first half. If Ayr thought this meant they were still in with a chance, those hopes were quickly extinguished. Just four minutes after half-time it was Smith at the double when he turned the ball home from close range after good build up play out wide.

The returning Kennedy was rarely involved in what was a relaxing reintroduction to the first team, and the only negative on the day was Rangers failing to turn their massive superiority into more goals. The 2-0 final score flattered the visitors, who seemed happy to just avoid a hammering. Wallace was fulsome in his praise of the team, particularly Forsyth who he described as 'probably the best centre-back in Britain right now'. He also looked forward with some confidence to the midweek trip to the Netherlands, and despite the goalless first leg he stated, 'I felt after the first leg with Twente we had a good chance of winning. That still stands.'

Wallace took a 16-man travelling party and didn't let a lengthy flight delay upset his optimism. The group didn't include the suspended Johnstone or the injured Greig, with Wallace emphasising in the pre-match press interviews the important role that the returning Derek Parlane had in leading the attack against a Dutch team in good form in their domestic league.

Much of the press focus before the game was on the behaviour of the travelling Rangers supporters, the match coming soon after Manchester United fans rioted in France at a tie against Saint-Étienne, causing their team to briefly be expelled from the tournament before the punishment was changed to playing the return match at a ground at least 200km from Manchester. With the recent trouble at Love Street, there were some reporters suggesting a Rangers defeat could see similar scenes. FC Twente seemed much more relaxed, with club official Gerrard Loubbers confirming they had no safety concerns and there would be no special segregation of supporters inside the Diekman Stadium. The local police were unwilling to take risks, however, and confirmed their plan to meet supporters' buses on the outskirts of the town and escort them to and from the ground.

FC Twente v Rangers
Wednesday, 28 September 1977, Diekman Stadium
Stewart Kennedy, Sandy Jardine, Alex Miller, Tom Forsyth, Colin Jackson, Alex MacDonald, Bobby McKean, Bobby Russell, Derek Parlane, Gordon Smith, Davie Cooper
Substitutes: Tommy McLean, Martin Henderson

There was only one change made from the weekend, the enforced return of Derek Parlane in place of Derek Johnstone. The Dutch hosts went with the same 11 as at Ibrox a fortnight before, coach Spitz Kohn content with how that match unfolded and his team's subsequent good form. Once Rangers had arrived to train at the stadium the day before the match, Wallace expressed concern at two aspects of the stadium that might unsettle his team. First, the floodlights were of poor quality, only just meeting UEFA standards for their competitions. Secondly, the playing surface measured a massive 80 yards wide, a full six yards wider than the big playing surface at Ibrox. He worried that these gave the home team a real advantage, and insisted on an extra training session the night before to try to get his players accustomed to both.

The wide-open spaces of their home pitch suited FC Twente, and from early on they showed the defensive setup from the first leg had been abandoned in favour of quick attacks down either flank. The Rangers defence was quickly under pressure, with Stewart Kennedy saving well from Ab Gritter in the first few minutes. It wasn't completely one way, however, Colin Jackson coming close with a header from a Sandy Jardine free kick in the seventh minute. But the play was mainly heading towards Kennedy and he was mighty relieved to see a flashing Arnold Muhren shot fizz inches wide. Forsyth then cleared an effort off the line with his goalkeeper beaten, as the small band of travelling Rangers fans began to fear the worst.

The pressure finally told after 34 minutes, and after some incisive and intelligent play from the home team the goal was a simple goalkeeping error. A Jaap Bos cross should have been easy for Kennedy, but he totally misjudged the flight of the ball and it soared over his outstretched arms. In behind him ran Gritter, who had a simple task to head it into the unguarded goal. Rangers were rocking and needed to get into the dressing room at half-time without conceding again. They failed to do so, when Muhren's thumping finish from a clever cut-back in the 40th minute made it 2-0 and gave them a huge mountain to climb. It could have been even worse, as seconds before the Austrian referee brought the half to an end Alex Miller seemed to handle in the box but no penalty was given.

Wallace tried to rally his beleaguered troops at the interval, but after a brief flurry at the start of the second half it was Twente who still looked by far the more dangerous side. Full-back Cedric van Ierssel came close with a ferocious shot that grazed the bar, and with midfielders Muhren and Frans Thijssen dominating the ball, a third goal looked a matter of time. It came with 25 minutes remaining, a Kick van der Vall 20-yarder that flew past Kennedy into the corner.

At 3-0 the match was over, and Twente could afford to relax somewhat. This allowed a late rally from Rangers and they got the perfect chance to grab some small consolation when referee Erich Linemayr awarded a late penalty after Smith went down in a challenge by goalkeeper André van

SEPTEMBER: THE COMEBACK

Gerven. Miller's spot-kick summed up the night; he shot weakly, straight at van Gerven, who saved easily.

In the end, a 3-0 defeat was an accurate reflection of the match, where a talented and perhaps underestimated Twente side were simply too good on the night for a Rangers team without John Greig or Derek Johnstone, and with inexperience in their midfield and attack. Twente showed they were no mugs by reaching the semi-finals of the competition, where they eventually lost out to eventual winners Anderlecht. Their midfield pair of Thijssen and Muhren would go on to become key players in the excellent Ipswich Town side under Bobby Robson who won the 1981 UEFA Cup.

Jock Wallace, although bitterly disappointed with the manner of the defeat, was philosophical afterwards. Referring to his new signings who had all played the full match, he said, 'Maybe just another month or so might have had us ready for that game.' His realism didn't fully overcome his anger, however, as he added, 'The players will be told in no uncertain manner what is expected of them. We have had some good displays this season, and some bad ones. But this was probably the worst. If we are to do anything, we must be consistent.'

September ended with Wallace still looking for that winning consistency. Rangers had enjoyed an incredible Old Firm victory and had played some sparkling football in the month. But they were dumped out of Europe and were still down in fourth in the league table, four points behind pacesetters Aberdeen. All at Ibrox hoped that October would see that gap closed and the winning habit found.

4

October: The Team Hits Top Gear

THE FIRST opponents of the new month were newly promoted Clydebank, who were struggling at the foot of the table and still coming to terms with the loss of their talisman Davie Cooper. It looked the perfect Ibrox match for the team to shake off the gloom of their European nightmare, and to score a few goals in front of their home crowd.

Jock Wallace resisted the temptation to make too many changes, settling with just the obvious one of bringing back Derek Johnstone up front. John Greig wasn't risked, with a huge cup tie in midweek against Aberdeen on the horizon.

Rangers v Clydebank
Saturday, 1 October 1977, Ibrox
Stewart Kennedy, Sandy Jardine, Alex Miller, Tom Forsyth, Colin Jackson, Alex MacDonald, Bobby McKean, Bobby Russell, Derek Johnstone, Gordon Smith, Davie Cooper
Substitutes: Tommy McLean, Derek Parlane

There were just under 15,000 inside Ibrox on a day that saw high winds in the Glasgow area. Clydebank elected to play with the wind at their backs in the first half towards the partially covered 'Rangers end', and with the elements in their favour the underdogs quickly gained territorial advantage. Bill Munro's team created several chances in a first half where Rangers often struggled to get out of their own half, Stewart Kennedy's goal kicks lucky to travel more than 35 yards.

Midfielder Gerry Colgan was the man who seemed at the centre of everything, and he had already missed a great chance when he gave the Bankies a deserved lead in the 21st minute. The Clydebank number 11 latched on to a headed clearance by Sandy Jardine to cleverly loft the ball into the roof of the net from 20 yards out. And by the time referee David Syme halted proceedings for half-time, Colgan had passed up a glorious chance to double the lead, missing the target when it was easier to score.

Despite the conditions, the Ibrox crowd were unforgiving as their team left the pitch and it was a totally transformed Rangers who took to the field after Wallace's words of encouragement. Now with the wind against them, it was Clydebank's turn to be camped in their own half, and within the first five minutes of the restart Rangers had passed up a couple of chances to level the scores. When the equaliser came in the 53rd minute it was a tale of two old team-mates. Clydebank number eight Billy McColl was a great friend of Davie Cooper, but when the visiting midfielder dallied on the ball 30 yards from goal his old pal temporarily put their friendship aside. Cooper nipped in, dispossessed McColl, then ran in on goal unopposed before slamming the ball past goalkeeper Jim Gallacher and into the net.

McColl slumped to the turf as Cooper celebrated, and from that moment on it was a case of how many. The Bankies' defence, with long-serving Jim Fallon at the heart, were now being overrun, and only a combination of careless finishing and smart goalkeeping prevented Rangers from quickly going in front. But when they conceded a free kick in a dangerous position in the 67th minute, it signalled the end of their resistance. Old boy Cooper was again the tormenter-in-chief, his wicked delivery being headed home by the diving Gordon Smith. As the former Kilmarnock man wheeled away to celebrate, it was now a question of how big the winning margin would be.

The answer to that was 4-1 as both goalscorers added to their tallies. Cooper's second of the match was something of a rarity, a wicked in-swinging corner that went into the net beyond Gallacher without any other player getting a touch. No doubt it had been wind-assisted, but even allowing for the elements it was a magnificently struck dead ball. Then in the final minute, Smith scored his tenth goal of a dream debut season when he turned in an Alex MacDonald free kick.

Munro bemoaned the final scoreline, saying, 'That was never a 4-1 game,' whereas Wallace focused on his team's second-half dominance by commenting, 'We got a fright in the first half, but I was delighted with the showing of the lads after half-time.'

With Aberdeen dropping a point at Motherwell, Dundee United went top of the table on goal difference from the Dons, with Rangers now in third place just three behind the pair from the north-east. Aberdeen were to visit Ibrox in midweek in the first leg of their long-awaited League Cup clash, a match many inside Ibrox were seeing as something of a revenge mission after several defeats to the Dons in recent times. The 5-1 League Cup semi-final drubbing the previous season and the 3-1 reverse on the opening day were both especially fresh in the memory.

OCTOBER: THE TEAM HITS TOP GEAR

On the Monday, Wallace started John Greig, Tommy McLean and Derek Parlane in the reserve team's win over Clydebank to give all three some match time prior to the cup tie. The next day, Wallace confirmed that McLean would return to the team against Aberdeen, describing his display for the reserves as 'magnificent'. He stated that the match was still too early for Greig to start, but he had a chance of being fit enough for a place on the bench.

Rangers v Aberdeen
Wednesday, 5 October 1977, Ibrox
Stewart Kennedy, Sandy Jardine, Alex Miller, Tom Forsyth, Colin Jackson, Alex MacDonald, Tommy McLean, Bobby Russell, Derek Johnstone, Gordon Smith, Davie Cooper
Substitutes: John Greig, Bobby McKean

There had been much speculation in the days before the tie that Aberdeen would be without their top scorer Joe Harper, manager Billy McNeill saying he was suffering from flu. But Harper took to the field in his usual position. The 25,000 crowd would witness a match that would live long in the memory.

McNeill got his expected hostile reception prior to kick-off, many fans not just remembering his long association with Celtic but also his celebrations at the final whistle on the season's opening day at Pittodrie. The players possibly hadn't forgotten that either, as they tore into Aberdeen straight from kick-off. The visitors were immediately under pressure as Rangers' quick passing and high intensity pushed them into defence. The supporters were enjoying this lightning start and they got their reward in just the third minute when Rangers scored. Full-back Miller overlapped on the left and sent in an excellent cross and there was Smith ghosting into the penalty area at the back post to direct his header beyond Bobby Clark.

Rangers were in no mood to lie back on their early lead, and the Dons goal had a charmed life as Tommy McLean forced a brilliant save from Clark before smashing a shot off the crossbar minutes later with the goalkeeper well beaten. Aberdeen were being swamped, although in a rare attack Drew Jarvie almost scored a totally undeserved equaliser but was denied by Sandy Jardine's goal-line clearance. It would have been a travesty if that had gone in, but then in the last 15 minutes of the half the scoreline was given a more accurate reflection of the match.

First, in the 31st minute Jardine and McLean combined down the right, and the winger's cross was brilliantly hooked into the net by Derek Johnstone. Most of the crowd would have settled for a 2-0 advantage at half-time – but not this rampant Rangers team.

Two minutes before the interval, a sublime McLean through ball found Smith running in on goal and the in-form forward found the Aberdeen net with a clever finish. Then, as referee George Smith was checking his watch to end the half, he instead found himself awarding a penalty to Rangers after Alex MacDonald was chopped down in the area by the beleaguered Willie Garner. The half-time score of 4-0 was completed when Miller confidently scored from the spot.

It had been as good a 45 minutes from Rangers as most fans in the ground could remember, and the tie looked all but over when McNeill dashed up the tunnel as the referee put his team temporarily out of their misery. With the memory of Aberdeen's humiliating 5-1 semi-final win the previous season, the fans hoped for an even bigger scoreline to complete their revenge. They got it.

OCTOBER: THE TEAM HITS TOP GEAR

It was maybe no great surprise that Rangers couldn't maintain the intensity of the first half, but they continued to dominate proceedings after the break, even if no longer creating as many clear chances. It took 25 minutes for number five to arrive but it was a goal worth waiting for. Bobby Russell, who had another majestic match in midfield, made another good forward run, and he was found by an inch-perfect Cooper pass. With the Aberdeen defence and goalkeeper rushing to Russell to try to prevent a shot, he instead showed his vision by picking out the unmarked Smith at the back post. Smith completed his first Rangers hat-trick in emphatic style.

At 5-0 Rangers seemed to take their foot off the pedal, and they got punished with ten minutes remaining as Aberdeen grabbed a consolation goal. It was a well-worked strike, Harper wrong footing the Rangers defence by dummying a John McMaster cross, allowing Duncan Davidson to run in behind him to slam the ball past Stewart Kennedy. It was now the reverse of the 5-1 scoreline from the previous season, but Rangers were determined to have the final say and to better that result. With just four minutes left a Cooper cross was headed beyond Clark by MacDonald and the final score read Rangers 6 Aberdeen 1. The ovation given to the team at the final whistle could be heard on the other side of the Clyde.

The press and pundits were united in describing this win as one of the best displays seen at Ibrox in a very long time. Every player had played their part, and with Russell, Cooper and McLean the creative force behind deadly goalscoring duo Smith and Johnstone, the team looked more potent, and more entertaining, than any Rangers team since the glory days of the 1960s. Wallace summed it up when telling the press, 'That was the best Rangers performance I have seen since I came here. We were fantastic.' His Aberdeen counterpart McNeill was the exact opposite, his dejected press interview starting with, 'Don't ask me how I'm feeling. You can guess.'

On the Friday, Wallace confidently announced an unchanged 11 would face league leaders Dundee United at Tannadice the following day. He also confirmed that striker Colin Stein had joined Kilmarnock on an initial three-month loan deal, the Ayrshire club needing a new centre-forward after the tragic death of their top goalscorer Ian Fallis in a road accident a few days earlier. Stein would forever be a legend at Ibrox, scoring the opener in the 1972 European Cup Winners' Cup Final in Barcelona five years earlier. He then cemented his status by hitting the goal that won the league title at Easter Road in 1975 in his second spell with the club, as the championship finally returned to Ibrox after 11 long years. He was now in the veteran stage of his career and well down the pecking order, so the move suited all parties.

Dundee United v Rangers
Saturday, 8 October 1977, Tannadice
Stewart Kennedy, Sandy Jardine, Alex Miller, Tom Forsyth, Colin Jackson, Alex MacDonald, Tommy McLean, Bobby Russell, Derek Johnstone, Gordon Smith, Davie Cooper
Substitutes: Bobby McKean, Martin Henderson

Although the starting 11 was the same as the midweek annihilation of Aberdeen, Wallace decided it would be better for John Greig's fitness that he played in the reserve fixture between the teams at Ibrox than sit on the bench again. The club captain gave his manager food for thought as he scored a hat-trick.

OCTOBER: THE TEAM HITS TOP GEAR

Meanwhile, at Tannadice there was a mood in the crowd that this was a vital fixture in the title race. The 19,000 attendance reflected that, with the big home support daring to dream that their unfancied young team under the management of Jim McLean could consolidate their position on top of the league table. The Rangers fans, however, were in confident mood after watching their side's devastating performance in midweek, and they were looking forward to McLean's youngest brother Tommy being the happier in the family at full time.

The first half demonstrated how good both defences were. United's central pairing of 23-year-old Paul Hegarty and 21-year-old David Narey stuck like glue to the Rangers strikers, while the vastly more experienced Tom Forsyth and Colin Jackson didn't allow frontmen Paul Sturrock and John Bourke an inch of room either. It meant that game became one of few chances, not helped by referee John Paterson having to stop play for several free kicks. The one player on the field who looked capable of finding space was Bobby Russell, who continued to look like the find of the season.

Neither team could claim an outstanding chance to score in an attritional first half. Perhaps the main surprise wasn't the blank scoreline, but the fact only one booking had been administered by Paterson, United's Derek Addison the only name taken despite some crunching tackles.

The second half saw slightly more football played, but defences continued to dominate. Jim McLean turned to his bench and introduced another of his young prospects, 19-year-old Billy Kirkwood replacing the veteran Gordon Wallace. But it was the visitors who were slowly taking control, Hamish McAlpine in the home goal finally being called into more serious action. Johnstone and Cooper had half chances that came to nothing, before the deadlock was broken with less than 20 minutes remaining. It was a goal fit to win any game.

Russell started it near the halfway line when he found Forsyth breaking forward. The big defender allowed Tommy McLean to take over, and he played it through to MacDonald who had found a yard of space near the edge of the United area. MacDonald played a delicious first-time pass on the volley into the path of Russell, who had kept on running. The young midfielder took one touch to control the ball, then thumped an unstoppable shot high into the net past McAlpine just as Narey threw himself into a last-gasp tackle.

It was a game that always looked like being settled by just one goal, and the massive away support behind the goal celebrated wildly. United threw on their other substitute, recent signing Bobby Robinson, as time began to run out on them. The Rangers defence were in no mood to allow the lead to slip, with the players and supporters wearing huge smiles when the final whistle sounded. The name chanted loudest was that of Bobby Russell, who had scored the only goal against the league leaders just a few months after he had been playing on the same Tannadice pitch in a trial match trying to impress enough to earn a Rangers contract.

Jock Wallace was delighted with the resolve of his team, remarking, 'It was a tight and tense match, but I thought we deserved the two points.' The result allowed Aberdeen to reclaim top spot in the table after an impressive win at Love Street, Rangers remaining in third place but now just a point behind United and three points off the summit. Meanwhile, Celtic incredibly lost for the fifth time in their opening eight fixtures, going down at Firhill. They already looked like they were incapable of mounting a serious title defence.

OCTOBER: THE TEAM HITS TOP GEAR

It had been a very good week for Rangers. With no midweek match due to Scotland's crunch World Cup qualifier against Wales, the players not on international duty could get some rest and look forward to another tough away trip the next Saturday, when Rangers were to play fourth-placed Motherwell at Fir Park.

John Greig's return to fitness was given a further boost on the Monday evening when he played in a Reserve Cup match against Dumbarton and scored the only goal. This good news paled into national insignificance two nights later as Scotland faced Wales in an all-or-nothing World Cup qualifier at Anfield in Liverpool. It was the Scots who were celebrating, a 2-0 win in front of a massive Tartan travelling support earning the country their place in the finals the following summer in Argentina and making manager Ally McLeod a national hero. On the pitch, Sandy Jardine and Tom Forsyth played their part in an unforgettable occasion, albeit Jardine suffered an injury and was replaced after an hour by Manchester United's Martin Buchan.

The country was on a high, but thoughts had to turn back to domestic football with some exciting-looking fixtures on the weekend. One Rangers player who wouldn't be appearing at Fir Park was 21-year-old centre-forward Martin Henderson, a hero of the 1975/76 treble season who was finding it difficult to command a place in the Ibrox attack. He agreed a three-month loan deal to join Hibs, meaning Jock Wallace had loaned out two strikers in the space of a week. A third departure was confirmed the next day, with Partick Thistle manager Bertie Auld successful in a £25,000 offer for reserve midfielder Alex O'Hara, the player happy to make the move in the search of regular first-team football.

There would also be no Jardine in the side that travelled to Motherwell; his ankle injury was not as bad as first feared, but with John Greig now back fully fit it represented a risk not worth taking.

Motherwell v Rangers
Saturday, 15 October 1977, Fir Park
Stewart Kennedy, John Greig, Alex Miller, Tom Forsyth, Colin Jackson, Alex MacDonald, Tommy McLean, Bobby Russell, Derek Johnstone, Gordon Smith, Davie Cooper
Substitutes: Bobby McKean, Ally Dawson

Many expected Greig to slot in at left-back, with Alex Miller switching across to fill Jardine's position on the right, but the manager decided on making just one alteration to a defence that had been superb at Tannadice, so the club skipper started in the right-back role. There must have been an element of doubt on Greig's ability to last the full match, with young defender Ally Dawson given his first place on the bench of the campaign.

It was another McLean family occasion, winger Tommy having faced the team managed by brother Jim the previous weekend and now coming up against the side managed by his other brother Willie. From early on, it was obvious that the youngest sibling would again be the man who would come out on top. Rangers immediately took control of the game, with the massive away support in the 20,000 crowd in full voice as they watched their team dominate. Motherwell did well to hold out for 14 minutes but the inevitable had to happen, even if the circumstances were slightly controversial.

Davie Cooper took possession and spotted Gordon Smith making a forward run. The winger's pass was perfection, allowing Smith a clear run in on goalkeeper Jim Muir.

The Motherwell fans and some of their players claimed offside but the flag remained down, allowing Smith to calmly lob the ball over the advancing Muir and into the net to continue his incredible scoring run since his arrival from Kilmarnock.

Smith was now the top scorer in domestic football among Premier Division players, but the rest of the first half was a reminder to everyone that he wasn't the only prolific goalscorer in royal blue. Ten minutes after the opener, Cooper was again the mastermind behind another Rangers goal. This time his wickedly flighted corner was headed on by Colin Jackson and despatched into the net by Derek Johnstone.

Johnstone had completed a hat-trick just nine minutes later. His second goal came after 28 minutes, a thumping shot from 15 yards that took a slight deflection but looked a scorer anyway. Then he scored the kind of goal he was perhaps most famous for, a towering header from a Tommy McLean corner. The match was only 33 minutes old, Rangers were 4-0 up, and they looked in the kind of mood that must have had the home support fearing an embarrassing afternoon.

Motherwell managed to get to half-time without further loss, and they were maybe lucky not to hear the booing of their own fans as it was drowned out by the huge cheers of travelling Rangers army. They were expecting more of the same after the interval, but their team seemed to drop several gears and looked more content to avoid injury and keep their opponents out than to inflict further misery on them. Tom Forsyth was again a rock at the heart of the defence, with his display winning most of the man of the match awards in the Monday newspapers despite the scoring heroics of Johnstone.

Willie McLean threw on both of his substitutes and one of them finally pulled a goal back, former Hibs man Jim O'Rourke finishing off after being set up by ex-Celtic player Vic Davidson. The 4-1 scoreline flattered the hosts, and it seemed to awaken Rangers again, with Smith missing two clear chances before the end. The result was a good one, and it became even better when news filtered through that leaders Aberdeen, second-placed Dundee United, and old rivals Celtic had all lost. Rangers were now up to second and just one point behind an Aberdeen team who were the visitors to Ibrox in seven days' time. A win would see the Gers sit top of the table for the first time in season 1977/78.

Despite such a devastating performance and the team's improving title chances, it was a furious Jock Wallace who spoke to reporters. 'The players were fantastic in the first half,' he said, 'but that standard must be maintained. If we can play like that in the first half then there is no excuse for not repeating it in the second. I was very angry at the way we played in the second half, and the players were left in no doubt how I feel.'

The following midweek was allocated to European competition, and with Rangers already eliminated it was instead used to finally play a fixture from the previous season. The 1976/77 Glasgow Cup had never been completed due to fixture congestion, with Celtic or Queens Park awaiting the winner of a semi-final between Rangers and Partick Thistle. It meant the bizarre possibility of players like Bobby Russell, Davie Cooper and Gordon Smith all winning a medal in a competition that was meant to have been completed before any of them had signed for the club.

Thistle were in excellent form, with recent wins over both Celtic and Dundee United, and with manager Bertie Auld a man who would enjoy a victory over Rangers more than most, Wallace opted to field a very strong 11. The only change saw Smith miss out; he had taken a knock at Fir Park and a fitness test suggested a few days' rest would be beneficial with the top-of-the-table clash with Aberdeen just days away. Auld confirmed that Alex O'Hara, his recent signing from Rangers, would make his first start for his new club.

Rangers v Partick Thistle
Tuesday, 18 October 1977, Ibrox
Stewart Kennedy, John Greig, Alex Miller, Tom Forsyth, Colin Jackson, Alex MacDonald, Billy MacKay, Bobby Russell, Derek Johnstone, Tommy McLean, Davie Cooper
Substitutes: Bobby McKean, Ally Dawson

Wallace opted to move Tommy McLean infield and to give another start to teenager Billy MacKay on the right wing. Despite the team's sparkling recent form, a crowd of only 10,000 decided to go and see the semi-final, perhaps another sign that the Glasgow Cup's place as a significant tournament was now in the past. Thistle fielded an equally strong line-up after Auld had spoken in his pre-match interviews about how his side saw this as a major opportunity to win silverware. His only significant player missing was Scotland goalkeeper Alan Rough, although his young deputy Billy Thomson had impressed in his previous starts and was regarded as a potential future international himself.

Despite it being his first start for the club, O'Hara was given the Thistle captaincy for the evening, a nod towards his time at Ibrox. Like the rest of his new teammates, he must have been wondering at half-time just how this Rangers team could be stopped. The small crowd saw Rangers take control early on with goalkeeper Thomson heavily involved. The crisp passing and intelligent forward play that had delighted home fans' support was again in evidence, although it took 26 minutes for the breakthrough. When it came it was a moment of individual brilliance. Greig tapped a short free kick to McLean, who then struck a delightful 25-yard shot into the top corner beyond the diving Thomson.

There was still almost an hour to play when the lead was doubled. This time it was a rare goal for Forsyth, whose recent displays had drawn huge praise from his club and country managers. The big centre-back galloped forward, played a clever one-two with goalscorer McLean, then smashed the ball low past Thomson. It was his first goal for just over three years, the last being against Morton in October 1974. It rounded off something of an exhibition-like first half with Rangers looking vastly superior and capable of increasing their goal tally if and when they wanted.

Wallace made a change at the interval, giving Johnstone an early night with the weekend in mind. Bobby McKean was the replacement, meaning Rangers now had no natural centre-forward in the team and were without both of their most potent goal threats with Smith already missing. Without a focal point in attack they struggled to recapture their first-half dominance, the visiting defence now able to snuff out the danger before their goal was under serious threat. Partick started to venture forward, sensing this wasn't the same challenge as the first half.

Although now a more even contest, Partick carried little real threat themselves, but that changed when Auld made a double substitution with 25 minutes to play. The new players combined five minutes later to shock the home support. Bobby Houston played an accurate free kick into the Rangers penalty box, and big striker Doug Somner bulleted a header past Stewart Kennedy. The atmosphere inside Ibrox changed, from coasting to the expected win the Rangers fans now sensed a potential upset.

And with 11 minutes remaining, their fears worsened. A Brian Whittaker free kick caused panic in the penalty area, the ball falling to Somner who lashed it into the net. Auld leapt for joy on the touchline as his substitute's second goal had given Thistle all the momentum. Both sides then tried to find a winner, but when referee Ian Foote signalled the end of 90 minutes it meant an immediate penalty shoot-out. The clubs had agreed there would be no replay or extra time, so the lottery of kicks from 12 yards would decide the winner.

The first six kicks were all scored, the Rangers men who hit the net being Miller, Russell and McLean. It was then advantage Rangers when Thistle's Jackie Campbell saw his effort saved by Kennedy. When Cooper then calmly slotted his penalty home, it meant that O'Hara had to score the final Partick kick or Rangers were through. The former Ibrox man could only shake his head in dismay when Kennedy pulled off another smart save; Rangers had won the shoot-out 4-3 and were in the final.

It was a final that would never happen – the competition was eventually abandoned when there were no suitable dates found for the remaining matches. Rangers weren't to know this at the time, but it seems strange to think this match was fitted in a season after it should have been played, then not seen as being important enough for the tournament to get completed.

The visit of Aberdeen on the Saturday was a hugely anticipated clash, the top two in the table going head-to-head, and with the added spice of the recent 6-1 mauling that Rangers had handed out in the League Cup to Billy McNeill's men. Jock Wallace confirmed on the Thursday that both Gordon Smith and Sandy Jardine were fit and available, and that Derek Johnstone was also fully fit having been taken off after 45 minutes against Partick as a precaution after complaining of a muscle strain. The threat of a suspension for Colin Jackson was also removed when he was censured by the SFA for four bookings during the season at their disciplinary meeting rather than given a ban. Rangers were the form side in Scotland, scoring a lot of goals, and now had all their top players available for the first time in the season. Similarly, McNeill declared he had all of his stars available for the match, and he spoke of his determination to put right the horrors of the League Cup drubbing.

Rangers v Aberdeen
Saturday, 22 October 1977, Ibrox
Stewart Kennedy, Sandy Jardine, John Greig, Tom Forsyth, Colin Jackson, Alex MacDonald, Tommy McLean, Bobby Russell, Derek Johnstone, Gordon Smith, Davie Cooper
Substitutes: Alex Miller, Derek Parlane

A healthy crowd of over 37,000 attended the biggest league game of the season so far, and they saw an afternoon full of controversy. Both teams seemed to be treating it like a cup tie, with neither midfield being given any time on the ball as the tackles flew in. Referee Hugh Alexander didn't help matters by initially allowing some meaty challenges to go unpunished, and by the time he decided to clamp down the tone had been set.

OCTOBER: THE TEAM HITS TOP GEAR

The first booking didn't arrive until the 28th minute, with Alexander becoming very much the centre of attention two minutes later. Tommy McLean ran into the Aberdeen penalty area where he was blocked off in a sandwich by two visiting defenders, prompting the referee to point to the spot. McNeill leapt from his dugout in anger, but it looked the right decision. Jardine ignored all the fuss and calmly slotted the ball past Bobby Clark to give Rangers the lead, and give the big home support reason to sing even louder.

If McNeill was angry after that, a few minutes later he was apoplectic. Cooper set off on a surging run with Aberdeen's Chic McLelland in hot pursuit. The full-back decided to crudely bring the winger down when he clearly wasn't going to catch him, Alexander producing a red card for a cynical and dangerous challenge. Mayhem ensued with the Aberdeen management in a fury as McLelland took the long walk off the pitch. There looked a real danger that the Dons' discipline would be lost completely, but just as the home fans were enjoying their serenading of McNeill the referee became a villain to both sides. Joe Harper went down in the Rangers penalty box, and the second spot-kick of the afternoon was awarded. The prolific little striker then picked himself up and confidently smashed home the equaliser. The teams left the pitch moments later, fans of both sides giving the man in the middle as much abuse as they could muster.

Although the scores were now level, Rangers had the advantage of an extra man, and most of their fans were confident that this would prove crucial in the second half. The players seemed to share that belief as Rangers dominated the early stages of the second period, with Bobby Russell particularly impressive. Aberdeen were hanging on and had goalkeeper Clark to thank when he saved another

Jardine penalty, Alexander's decision to award a third spot-kick of the match being accepted by all involved as the correct call this time.

Then, with 20 minutes left, the Aberdeen resistance was finally broken. A sweeping move involving four Rangers players ended with the ball being swept in from just a few yards out by Smith after the Dons' defence had been ripped open. The crowd were still celebrating just three minutes later when Johnstone intelligently chested down a high ball back into the path of MacDonald, and the midfield man struck a delightful low, swerving shot from 20 yards that had Clark beaten all the way.

At 3-1 up and with their opponents down to ten men, Rangers could now relax. To their credit, Aberdeen tried to battle, and Harper was unlucky to see a header hit the post with Kennedy beaten. That was their last hope of an unlikely comeback, and when Alexander's whistle ended the contest Rangers were top of the league.

Needless to say, in a game that saw five bookings, three penalties and a red card, the managers had contrasting opinions. McNeill refused to rule out his club sending a letter of complaint to the SFA, claiming his players had been 'scared to tackle' due to the referee's handling of the match. Wallace was typically blunt in his response, saying, 'I didn't see the referee score any goals or make any bad tackles. We won the game on merit, and I am delighted with the way my men played.'

Typically after such a contentious contest, the teams had to face each other again just four nights later with the second leg of their League Cup tie at Pittodrie to be completed. With a handsome lead, Wallace suggested that a couple of his fringe players would travel north, and he might give them some game time. In his pre-match press interviews the day before the match, Wallace hinted that one of his usual starters had picked up an injury in training, but refused to divulge his identity. He wanted to leave his opposite number guessing, but it would mean at least one change from the weekend.

He also confirmed that the players would have an overnight stop on the way back south at St Andrews, where the team would relax and play some golf before returning to Ibrox on Friday to prepare for another tough looking away league match at Easter Road.

Aberdeen v Rangers
Wednesday, 26 October 1977, Pittodrie
Stewart Kennedy, Sandy Jardine, Alex Miller, Tom Forsyth, John Greig, Alex MacDonald, Tommy McLean, Bobby Russell, Derek Johnstone, Gordon Smith, Davie Cooper
Substitutes: Bobby McKean, Derek Parlane

The mystery injury was now confirmed to be Colin Jackson, meaning Alex Miller returned to the team at left-back and John Greig moved inside to centre-half. Otherwise, the manager had opted to play his strongest side, with the fringe players mentioned as potential starters now just going along for the golf the following day! Aberdeen also decided to go with their best 11, with the majority of the 15,000 Pittodrie crowd hoping to see their team salvage some pride rather than expecting a miracle.

With the tie seemingly over the travelling support wasn't as big as it had been for other recent matches in Aberdeen, but those who did make the journey enjoyed the opening stages, spending their time mainly taunting the opposition fans and manager over the first-leg scoreline. And when the opening 20 minutes were safely negotiated, the attempts at defiance from the Aberdeen support in retaliation grew increasingly quiet.

McNeill had stated before the game that his team needed a fast start and to score first. It took half an hour for the deadlock to be broken, and when it happened it signalled the end for McNeill's faint hopes. The first leg's hat-trick hero, Gordon Smith, pounced on a loose ball at the edge of the Aberdeen area and drove a vicious shot past Clark to make the aggregate score 7-1 and to send the band of visiting fans into even greater voice.

It was perhaps natural that Rangers would now ease off, there was no way they could fail to get through now. Their passing became slack and their tackling slightly less intense, and they were punished for this in the 39th minute when midfielder Joe Smith was given too much room in the penalty area, unleashing a tremendous shot that flew past Kennedy and into the net off the post. The Rangers fans treated this as a minor inconvenience, and they remained in good voice until referee George Smith ended the opening half with the scores on the night level at 1-1.

The home support remained subdued, until their team scored again on 59 minutes. Drew Jarvie had scored a crucial double on the opening day of the season in Aberdeen's 3-1 win, and he was again on target as he hit a fine finish into the net from a Jim Shirra pass. At last the Dons fans had something to use as a reply to Rangers' taunting – their team were winning the match. Just five minutes later the noise from the majority of the crowd got considerably louder when Jarvie scored again, tucking the ball into the net as the Rangers defence hesitated.

Surely it was too late with three more goals still needed and only 25 minutes to play. Wallace decided to change things at the back; the defending for both second half goals had been abysmal. He took off Alex Miller, moved John Greig to left-back, brought Derek Johnstone back into centre-half, and brought on Derek Parlane up front. This switch settled Rangers back down, Johnstone again showing his amazing versatility at both ends of the field. The Aberdeen support gradually quietened as time ran out on their League Cup campaign. Rangers made one more change near the end, giving Bobby McKean the last few minutes and taking off Smith.

The 3-1 result matched the scoreline on that opening day, but the reaction to it was very different. McNeill spoke only of his team having restored some pride, while Wallace declared himself satisfied with going through, even if not totally happy with how the team had played in the second half.

On the Friday, the manager confirmed that Colin Jackson had shrugged off his injury and was available for Easter Road, and stated that the day spent in St Andrews had refreshed his players and they were raring to go as they looked to consolidate their position at the head of the league table. Wallace also found out that his team had been paired with Second Division Dunfermline in the quarter-finals of the League Cup, a draw that did nothing to change the bookmakers' odds on Rangers as hot favourites for the competition. That was for the future, however, with Wallace focused on defeating Hibs, the team who had won at Ibrox on the second Saturday of the season to prompt the now-forgotten chants from the supporters for the manager to go.

Hibs v Rangers
Saturday, 29 October 1977, Easter Road
Stewart Kennedy, Sandy Jardine, John Greig, Tom Forsyth, Colin Jackson, Alex MacDonald, Tommy

McLean, Bobby Russell, Derek Johnstone, Gordon Smith, Davie Cooper
Substitutes: Alex Miller, Bobby McKean

This would be a quick chance for the discarded Martin Henderson to show Wallace that he should still have a future at Ibrox, the on-loan centre-forward chosen to lead the line for the home team. A massive travelling support would also see Henderson up against their heroes, with an estimated 15,000 Rangers fans in the crowd of 22,000.

Henderson wasn't involved much in the early action as Rangers settled the quicker and put sustained pressure on the Hibs defence. With Bobby Russell and Davie Cooper again looking full of confidence, they created several decent openings. Smith and Johnstone both came close, but as the half wore on Hibs gradually inched their way back into the contest. The main moment of controversy came inside the Rangers penalty area when the home players and supporters loudly claimed for a spot-kick after the ball seemed to strike the arm of a defender as it flashed across the box, and in the resulting melee Tony Higgins crashed to the ground when challenging for the loose ball with Tom Forsyth. Referee John Paterson waved away their appeals on both occasions.

Johnstone was particularly unlucky not to see his name on the scoresheet when he saw a goal-bound header cleared off the line, but neither side was able to find the opener by the time the referee signalled the end of an increasingly frantic first half.

The pattern remained the same after the teams resumed battle, and both Smith and Russell should have done better when goalkeeper Mike McDonald was stranded out of position as Rangers continued to look the more likely. It always looked like one goal would settle the match, and the decisive moment arrived with 20 minutes remaining. Again it was Russell who was involved in the heart of the action. He picked up possession and drove into the Hibs penalty box, only to be tripped right on the edge by home forward Ally MacLeod. The Hibs man was adamant that the offence had happened just outside of the box, but referee Paterson was in no doubt and pointed to the penalty spot. Once the complaints had died down, Sandy Jardine remained the calmest man on the pitch to slot home the kick.

Johnstone had the chance to kill off the match soon afterwards with a header, but Rangers then had to survive some furious home pressure in the closing stages. Henderson almost came back to haunt his employers when he hit the post, and Wallace looked a relieved man when the final whistle sounded. It was the kind of 1-0 away win that champions need to grind out, and when news filtered through from Pittodrie that Aberdeen had been held 1-1 by lowly Clydebank the day got even better. Rangers now enjoyed a two-point cushion at the summit.

Wallace praised his team and their army of followers after the match, saying, 'The fans and players seem to be really together just now, and it is paying off on and off the field.' With a rare free midweek for the players to come due it being allocated to European fixtures, he could look forward to another challenging fixture at Ibrox in seven days. Visitors Partick Thistle had just beaten Dundee United to register a fourth successive league win, and the team who came so close to beating Rangers in the recent Glasgow Cup tie were now up to fourth place in the table, just four points behind the leaders.

One Rangers player did have an eventful midweek, with Gordon Smith attending a graduation ceremony at Glasgow College of Technology to receive his Bachelor of Arts degree in Business Studies. Despite his amazing goalscoring start at

Ibrox, Smith had eyes on a career after football. Meanwhile, closest title rivals Aberdeen strengthened their playing pool by signing midfielder Gordon Strachan from Dundee. The Dons were now back in second place, but they still had genuine hopes of returning to the top.

5

November: John Greig MBE

IN NOVEMBER 1977, the UK was in the grip of industrial action by power workers which saw electricity cuts across all nations. On Saturday, 5 November, several football matches kicked off earlier than usual at 2.30pm to reduce the need for floodlights, although Rangers' game with Partick Thistle at Ibrox wasn't one of them. A good crowd of over 28,000 were inside the stadium to see the two form teams in the division face each other.

Rangers v Partick Thistle
Saturday, 5 November 1977, Ibrox
Stewart Kennedy, Sandy Jardine, John Greig, Tom Forsyth, Colin Jackson, Alex MacDonald, Tommy McLean, Bobby Russell, Derek Parlane, Gordon Smith, Davie Cooper
Substitutes: Alex Miller, Chris Robertson

After declaring he would be picking an unchanged team to the press the day before, Jock Wallace was forced into a change up front when Derek Johnstone picked up an injury in training and failed a fitness test on the morning of the match. He had a more than able deputy to call on in the shape of Scotland international Derek Parlane, who must have been desperate to stake his claim for a more regular start.

Bertie Auld's interviews in the build-up to the game had been full of confidence, the Firhill manager promising the Ibrox crowd they would see an attacking Thistle who would be looking to win. And his team backed up those words with action, the visitors tearing out of the traps to silence the home fans. With former Rangers midfielder Alex O'Hara pulling the strings, they dominated early proceedings and incredibly found themselves two goals in front with only a quarter of an hour played. The Rangers defence were posted missing in the 13th minute, allowing big centre-forward Doug Somner plenty of time to knock home the opener. Then less than two minutes later, it was the turn of his strike partner Jim Melrose to beat Stewart Kennedy from close range.

Auld punched the air in delight as the Rangers support struggled to comprehend what they were watching. Their team looked disorganised and wide open, and they badly needed to get back into the game quickly. Within five minutes of going 2-0 behind, they did just that. Davie Cooper took possession on the left and sent across a wicked in-swinging cross, and there was Parlane rising between two Thistle defenders to bullet a low header past Scotland goalkeeper Alan Rough and into the net. The big striker looked delighted to be back among the goals, and he was looking sharp on his comeback.

The Thistle goal survived until half-time, with the home crowd sounding somewhat anxious when referee Bill Anderson signalled the end of an entertaining 45 minutes. That anxiety turned to roars of approval when Rangers equalised within three minutes of the restart. It was a virtual carbon copy of the first goal, an-inch perfect Cooper cross despatched into the net by the head of Parlane. Everyone in the ground thought that the comeback would now be completed, but nobody told Thistle and just two minutes later they were back in front.

O'Hara was again heavily involved, showing a combination of skill and desire to get the ball to the byline and cross low into the area. It dropped to the boot of midfielder Ian Gibson who poked the ball past the diving Kennedy to stun the stadium. Rangers had to climb the mountain all over again, and this was proving to be a difficult task with the Thistle defence superbly organised, full-back Brian Whittaker seemingly appearing everywhere as he cleared the danger several times.

Wallace threw on an extra forward in Chris Robertson as the clock became the Ibrox enemy, and it wasn't until the 80th minute that a point was saved by a man who could always be relied on to come up with an important goal. It wasn't the prettiest of strikes, but Alex MacDonald wasn't caring as he thumped the ball past Rough after a scramble in the six-yard box saw players of both teams desperately try to win the ball.

A breathless match ended 3-3; honours even and both teams probably happy with the outcome. Wallace was fulsome in his praise for the Maryhill outfit, declaring that he was happy to take a point from a match that Rangers could easily have lost. With Aberdeen winning, the gap at the top was back to a single point with Rangers now due to visit Parkhead for the second Old Firm match of the season. But first, Wallace had to focus his men on a League Cup quarter-final against Dunfermline at Ibrox.

One of the newspapers ran a story the day before the Dunfermline match that Kilmarnock wanted John Greig as their new manager. Both the captain and his boss laughed this off, insisting that their only priority was to bring silverware back to Ibrox. Wallace also confirmed that Derek Johnstone was back to fitness and would definitely play against the Fifers to give him match sharpness ahead of the big derby clash at the weekend.

Rangers v Dunfermline Athletic
Wednesday, 9 November 1977, Ibrox
Stewart Kennedy, Sandy Jardine, John Greig, Tom Forsyth, Colin Jackson, Alex MacDonald, Tommy McLean, Bobby Russell, Derek Johnstone, Gordon Smith, Davie Cooper
Substitutes: Alex Miller, Derek Parlane

Derek Parlane must have felt hard done by to be dropped again after his two-goal return in the previous game, but most of the 10,000 crowd agreed with the manager's decision to put Johnstone straight back in. They were expecting a straightforward night against the Second Division outfit, even more so after seeing a full-strength Rangers line-up.

On a wet and miserable night, Rangers tried to warm up their fans with a fast start, laying siege to the Dunfermline goal. Within the first two minutes Johnstone had almost marked his return with a goal, his header hitting the top of the bar with goalkeeper Hugh Whyte well beaten. Tom Forsyth, Gordon Smith and Bobby Russell all had their chance to open the scoring in the first 20 minutes, but the Fifers managed to somehow keep the score blank. It was Russell who came closest, Whyte touching his attempted lob on to the crossbar. The match was then stopped for a few minutes after Colin Jackson received a nasty head knock, with the big defender being patched up and playing on sporting a huge bandage. It didn't seem to affect him and in the 34th minute it was Jackson himself who finally broke the deadlock.

It was a goal that featured three of the back four. Sandy Jardine played a clever pass to Greig, who then sent a deep cross into the Dunfermline penalty area. Jackson had stayed forward from a previous attack, and he leapt highest to direct a header beyond Whyte. The goal was no more than Rangers had deserved for their almost complete domination, and the half-time scoreline took on a more accurate look when they doubled the lead just before the interval. Smith played a pass to Tommy McLean, who had wandered infield from his usual right-wing position. The little winger took two strides before lashing a deadly accurate 20-yard shot low into the corner.

Dunfermline manager Harry Melrose went up the tunnel moments later cursing his luck; things had looked so much different just ten minutes earlier when his team were bravely holding out. They tried to get forward a bit more after the break, although rarely troubling Stewart Kennedy. One more goal would likely kill the tie and with 20 minutes left it was that man McLean who again found the way through. He took a long Tom Forsyth pass in his stride, moved inside a defender and lofted a delightful chip over Whyte and into the net.

Rangers eased off, and they paid the price for slackness in the closing stages. Pars substitute Jim Mullin played a neat one-two at the edge of the penalty box before firing a shot past Kennedy to close the gap back to two goals with 12 minutes still to play. Then in the dying seconds, Mullin again broke into the box only to see Kennedy pull off an excellent stop. Referee Eddie Pringle blew for full time shortly afterwards, with Rangers in a commanding 3-1 lead after the first leg but kicking themselves that they still had some work to do to confirm their place in the last four.

Wallace singled out Tommy McLean for praise after his man-of-the-match display, and he also confirmed that all 11 players had come through unscathed and were available for the trip to the east end of Glasgow. His Celtic counterpart didn't have such good news to report, Jock Stein telling the press after their quarter-final first leg win over St Mirren that midfielder Tommy Burns had no chance of playing after suffering an ankle injury.

Two days before the match, both clubs were represented at a meeting with UEFA to discuss an idea of restructuring European club competitions into a league format rather than a straight knockout which was how all three European tournaments were organised at that time. The suggestion of two 24-team competitions with teams divided into groups of four who all played each other home and away didn't seem to excite either Celtic director Jimmy Farrell or Rangers vice-chairman Willie Waddell. The Ibrox response was a short 'it is a big project and needs more thinking about'.

Rangers enjoyed a seven-point lead over Celtic going into the Saturday match, making it much more important for the home side to win than the visitors. With the now customary 1pm kick-off time, there was an expectant crowd of 56,000 inside Parkhead when the teams entered the field, with the big Rangers support the more confident of victory.

Celtic v Rangers
Saturday, 12 November 1977, Celtic Park
Stewart Kennedy, Sandy Jardine, John Greig, Tom Forsyth, Colin Jackson, Alex MacDonald, Tommy McLean, Bobby Russell, Derek Johnstone, Gordon Smith, Davie Cooper
Substitutes: Alex Miller, Derek Parlane

Wallace seemed to have little thinking to do before naming his team, an unchanged line-up having been confirmed the day before the game. Stein gave an Old Firm debut to his recent signing from Ayr United, full-back Joe Filippi. There was also a place for ex-Rangers hero Alfie Conn, giving the visiting fans a villain to jeer for the afternoon. The referee was Eddie Anderson, whose name would feature heavily in the match reports to follow.

Despite their lowly position in the table, Celtic supporters had gone into the match buoyed by a run of better recent domestic form, but they feared the worst as Rangers quickly took control of the play. Conn, along with the rest of the Celtic forwards, hardly got a kick of the ball in the opening half an hour as the Rangers midfield totally overshadowed their opponents. With the ball-winning of MacDonald combined with the skill and poise of McLean and Russell, the match was one-way traffic. Celtic's best players were their overworked central defenders Roddie MacDonald and Jóhannes Eðvaldsson, who manfully repelled attack after attack with Rangers not troubling goalkeeper Peter Latchford as often as their possession merited.

But the dam had to burst, and the goal came in the 26th minute. Davie Cooper picked up possession wide on the left after a long Kennedy clearance caused confusion between Eðvaldsson and Filippi. The winger took full advantage, racing past the full-back and sliding the ball low across the Celtic six-yard line. In the middle the deadly Derek Johnstone got to the ball in front of MacDonald to flick the ball past the goalkeeper.

Many in the ground must have thought this was the start of a Rangers procession, but to their credit Celtic then stirred into life. For the first time Rangers had some defending to do, and they had Kennedy to thank for protecting their lead when he produced a magnificent diving save to tip a Ronnie Glavin free kick over the bar. When Anderson ended the opening half, Celtic seemed to have the forward momentum, and Wallace must have been regretting his team only having the one goal to show for the long period of dominance.

His fears were realised just five minutes into the second half when Celtic equalised. A Joe Craig headed knock-down fell perfectly for Tom McAdam, and he gave Kennedy no chance with a firm finish from around 12 yards. Rangers were on the ropes as the big home crowd urged their team forward, and just three minutes later came the first of the incidents that had Stein complaining in his post-match interviews.

Anderson blew for a Celtic free kick for a late tackle, before the ball broke to Colin Jackson. The defender played a terrible back-pass that was never reaching his goalkeeper, and in nipped McAdam to slide the ball into the net. The Rangers defence could rightly point to the fact that play had been stopped for several seconds before Kennedy was beaten and they therefore hadn't properly defended the situation, but this didn't prevent mass protests from the Celtic players who claimed they should have been given the advantage instead of a free kick a long way from goal.

Flair players Cooper, Russell and McLean had now disappeared from the game, as it became a desperate rearguard action by the Ibrox men. In the 62nd minute Celtic probably had a more justifiable cause for complaint when Craig went down in the penalty box under a strong Tom Forsyth tackle. It could easily have been a penalty but Anderson gave a corner, deciding that Forsyth had played the ball before the man. Celtic captain Andy Lynch was booked for his furious protestations as the home fans were in uproar. This started a brief spell where the discipline of both sides seemed to be lost, culminating in a bizarre booking for McLean who appeared to pretend to kick out at Johnny Doyle who was a good five yards away from him, the Celtic player then looking stunned as McLean's boot flew off and narrowly missed his head!

When football again broke out, it was Rangers who ended the game the stronger and created two decent chances in the closing minutes. First Latchford did well to stop an MacDonald shot, then MacDonald burst into the box unmarked but McLean's pass was overhit and the Celtic goalkeeper was able to collect the ball before the midfielder. A 1-1 draw was probably a fair result on the balance of the 90 minutes, in a classic 'game of two halves'. John Greig summed Rangers' reaction up when he told reporters, 'It's another tough away game out of the road and it keeps us seven points ahead of them.'

Greig had an important appointment before the midweek League Cup return tie with Dunfermline at East End Park. He had been awarded an MBE in The Queen's birthday honours list in the summer, and Tuesday, 15 November was the day he travelled to Buckingham Palace to meet Her Majesty. It was a memorable day for both, with the skipper pictured alongside wife Jeanette and son Murray outside the palace with his medal, while The Queen was receiving the news that she had become a grandmother for the first time as Princess Anne had given birth to a son.

On the same day, Rangers announced their annual results, with a profit of just over £78,000 recorded in the accounts for the previous year, giving the club over £224,000 available cash. With such financial progress, a dividend of 6.6 per cent per share was to be paid to shareholders.

It wasn't all good news, however. The latest meeting of the SFA disciplinary committee handed down a shock 24-day suspension to Tom Forsyth for his red card earlier in the season at Love Street. This was by far the longest suspension of all the cases they had looked at, and the news was treated with amazement at Ibrox as it far exceeded even the most pessimistic predictions. As things stood, the ban meant Forsyth could play at Dunfermline then he would miss all games until mid-December, which would include the League Cup semi-final and the final if Rangers got there, as it was due to be played on 10 December.

The weather in Dunfermline would surely have kept away any supporters uncertain on leaving the house, with driving rain and spells of sleet and snow. After putting on his Sunday best to meet The Queen just 24 hours earlier, this was a definite return to reality for John Greig!

Dunfermline Athletic v Rangers
Wednesday, 16 November 1977, East End Park
Stewart Kennedy, Sandy Jardine, John Greig, Tom Forsyth, Colin Jackson, Alex MacDonald, Tommy McLean, Bobby Russell, Derek Johnstone, Gordon Smith, Davie Cooper
Substitutes: Alex Miller, Bobby McKean

Jock Wallace decided on another unchanged 11, but rewarded winger Bobby McKean with a place on the bench after good recent displays in the reserves. The 8,500 crowd was the biggest seen in East End Park for many years, despite the horrendous conditions. The teams would be playing on a mudheap of a surface, which was made all the more treacherous as puddles were forming due to the incessant rain. It certainly wasn't a night for the football purist.

NOVEMBER: JOHN GREIG MBE

The Rangers fans had a new chant for the evening, with the sound of 'John Greig MBE' being sung every time the team captain was anywhere near the ball. Although conditions made it near impossible, both sides tried their best to play passing football, with Tommy McLean somehow still able to find team-mates with precision. In the 14th minute his dead-ball skills created the opening goal, and it was inevitable who would score it. McLean's free kick was sent into the Pars' penalty area with menace, and in rampaged Greig MBE to send a first-time, side-footed finish past goalkeeper Hugh Whyte.

The hero of the day had given his public the moment they had wanted and the captain was mobbed by his team-mates. Now 4-1 up on aggregate, the tie looked over, but the lower-league team refused to throw in the towel and went in search of an equaliser on the night. They gave the Rangers defence a couple of anxious moments before a Bobby Robertson cross was headed superbly past Stewart Kennedy by the unmarked Bobby Morrison. The home crowd were delirious, but their dreams of a major upset were almost immediately ended when just a minute later Davie Cooper was brought down in the area by right-back Jim Scott. Eddie Pringle awarded the penalty, and Sandy Jardine restored the three-goal aggregate advantage.

The priority for the crowd at half-time was avoiding hypothermia as the rain turned to snow. The players in the second half tried manfully to keep them entertained, or maybe just to keep themselves heated up. Tom Forsyth had to leave the pitch just after the hour after a clash with Jim Meakin saw blood pouring from a leg wound. The ironman defender would need five stitches, and would have been doubtful to play in the next match if he hadn't received his suspension.

The main two remaining talking points both centred around Derek Johnstone. He was blatantly fouled in the area when running on to a through ball, but Pringle decided one spot-kick was quite enough for the night. Then in the 78th minute, the centre-forward got his head on a typically perfect Cooper cross to score the third Rangers goal of the evening, and to match the first leg score of 3-1.

The 6-2 aggregate win was a fair reflection of the gulf between the teams, with Wallace saying afterwards, 'I thought we played a lot of good football in the conditions. I was pleased with the team, they did well.' He also said that he hadn't yet decided how he would reshape his defence to compensate the loss of Forsyth; he had a couple of options to consider. The draw for the semi-finals saw Rangers paired with another Second Division team, little Forfar Athletic, who had enjoyed a fairytale run in the competition under their player-manager Archie Knox. The tie was to be played on Monday, 28 November at Hampden.

Attention then turned to the weekend league fixture, a visit to Ibrox by Alex Ferguson's exciting young St Mirren team who had played out a thrilling 3-3 draw with Rangers earlier in the season in Paisley.

Rangers v St Mirren
Saturday, 19 November 1977, Ibrox
Stewart Kennedy, Sandy Jardine, Alex Miller, John Greig, Colin Jackson, Alex MacDonald, Tommy McLean, Bobby Russell, Derek Johnstone, Gordon Smith, Davie Cooper
Substitutes: Derek Parlane, Bobby McKean

Wallace had decided to move Greig into central defence and bring in Alex Miller at left-back, rather than disrupt the forward line by dropping Johnstone back to centre-half.

The 25,000 crowd didn't have the midweek East End Park rain and snow to contend with, but there was a stiff wind blowing down the pitch that favoured the visitors in the first half.

It took some time for both teams to get used to the blustery conditions, but once the game settled down it developed into an even and entertaining contest. Rangers looked the more accomplished team, but despite the clever passing of Russell and Cooper they struggled to fashion any really clear openings. Likewise, Saints enjoyed several promising positions in and around the Rangers area using a more direct brand of football, but Kennedy had nothing especially difficult to deal with.

The match looked to be heading for half-time without any big talking points apart from a good Rangers penalty claim when John Young handled in his penalty area, but that all changed in the very last minute of the half. In what must have been the most uneven looking fight ever, the diminutive figure of Tommy McLean got involved in an off-the-ball altercation with visiting centre-half Bobby Reid, the pair trading blows despite the winger being almost a foot shorter than his opponent. It wasn't entirely clear what started the argument, but linesman Harry Kerrigan was unimpressed and brought it to the attention of referee David Syme. The incident took an even stranger twist as the referee sent McLean from the field along with the totally innocent Andy Dunlop, only for Syme to realise his mistake, signal for Dunlop to return to the field, then send off Reid instead.

The crowd were still trying to make sense of it all when the half-time whistle sounded, giving the managers ten minutes to reshape their ten-man teams, and giving the spectators ten minutes to decide whether the players or the officials were more brainless. When the depleted teams resumed battle, the loss of a defensive lynchpin looked to be more significant as Rangers took the lead within a minute. Reid had been the man given the task of keeping the shackles on Johnstone, and the big striker took advantage of his new freedom by rising unmarked to head home a Cooper corner.

The home team went for the kill after this, sensing that St Mirren were still bedding in their new defensive unit. It really should have been 2-0 a few minutes later when Cooper sped through the defence and into the penalty area, but as he was about to shoot, team-mate Gordon Smith elected to take over but overran the ball and was crowded out. The Paisley men took full advantage of this let-off in the 66th minute when in a rare attack they shocked the Ibrox faithful by scoring a terrific equaliser. Frank McGarvey cut a low ball back across the Rangers box where it found midfielder Billy Stark. His low shot from the edge of the area was deadly accurate, beating Kennedy as it arrowed into the corner.

Former Rangers player Alex Ferguson leapt from his dugout in delight, but his joy turned to anger nine minutes later. Derek Parlane had been introduced in place of Smith as Rangers hunted for a winner, and he went crashing in the penalty area under a challenge from John Young. Syme had no hesitation in giving the penalty, sparking fruitless protests from Paisley players and management. Alex Miller ignored the fuss and calmly sent goalkeeper Donald Hunter the wrong way to give Rangers a lead they then never looked like relinquishing.

Ferguson must have calmed down by the time he spoke to the newspapers after the match, as he only said, 'The referee showed good control. After the sending-off incident the game might have exploded, but it didn't and that was due to the referee.' Wallace preferred to focus on another hard-fought win for his team, and the fact Rangers now enjoyed a three-point lead at the top of the table after closest rivals Aberdeen had lost 3-2 at Parkhead. The supporters were going to enjoy their Saturday night. The team had a free midweek but then were due to play twice in just three days, with a Saturday trip to Somerset Park to face Ayr in the league followed by a Monday night cup semi-final against Forfar at Hampden.

Wallace gave his team a vote of confidence on the Friday by telling the press he would name an unchanged side for the Ayrshire trip. He reported that Tom Forsyth had the stitches removed from his leg and should be fit to resume his season as soon as his 24-day suspension was over.

Ayr United v Rangers
Saturday, 26 November 1977, Somerset Park
Stewart Kennedy, Sandy Jardine, Alex Miller, John Greig, Colin Jackson, Alex MacDonald, Tommy McLean, Bobby Russell, Derek Johnstone, Gordon Smith, Davie Cooper
Substitutes: Derek Parlane, Bobby McKean

There were over 15,000 packed into the small seaside stadium for the visit of the leaders on a freezing cold afternoon. The pitch, although playable, would represent an extra challenge for the players, with one shaded wing being hard and slippery, while the other side benefited from some weak winter sunshine to thaw out much more.

The home team looked fired up for the occasion, and their midfielder Gordon Crammond had a couple of presentable chances in the opening period. But by the time the half-hour mark had come and gone, the best two chances had been passed up by Rangers. The usually deadly Johnstone amazed everyone by missing an open goal from eight yards, and Ayrshire boy Smith also should have buried an easy opportunity but fluffed his lines. In a match played in a cup-tie atmosphere, it looked as if the fans would enjoy their half-time refreshments without seeing a goal. Then in the 44th minute came the moment when the match was decided.

Enjoying the better side of the pitch in the first half, Tommy McLean took possession and whipped in a teasing cross. Not for the first time, it found the head of Johnstone, and not for the last time the striker guided the ball past Hugh Sproat and into the net. The Ayr players looked deflated, and as they trudged off the pitch at half-time they looked like a team who didn't believe they could recover from the blow. The second half was to prove that suspicion right.

From the first blast of Tommy Muirhead's whistle until the referee ended the contest 45 minutes later, Rangers battered their opponents and showed little mercy. Johnstone was the man who doubled the lead, scoring with yet another header in the 64th minute. This time the ball was delivered by the other winger; Cooper now roaming down the softer side of the Somerset surface. And within four minutes Sproat was picking the ball out of his net again. It was a finish that would never win any goal of the season contest, an almighty goalmouth melee which eventually saw Colin Jackson thumping it into the net.

United manager Alex Stuart was powerless to do anything but suffer the remaining minutes, and he suffered twice more. Johnstone completed his treble with 15 minutes to play following another Cooper delivery, this time dispatched low and hard by the centre-forward's left boot. Wallace had the luxury of giving both substitutes some time on the pitch in the closing minutes and they combined beautifully with five minutes remaining. Bobby McKean was the creator and Derek Parlane the man who got his name on the scoresheet.

A 5-0 rout was complete, and there were further smiles in the visiting dressing room when news filtered through from Firhill that Partick Thistle had beaten Aberdeen, meaning the Maryhill men were now in second place, and the gap to fourth-placed Aberdeen was now five points. Wallace praised the ruthlessness of his team, but also pointed out that they had another match just 48 hours later, and his attention was already fully on the challenge of Forfar at Hampden.

That challenge would need to wait as the semi-final was postponed early on the Monday afternoon, the frost on the playing surface combined with a freezing fog in the area making the decision an easy one, especially as it avoided the part-timers travelling down from the north-east. The match was rescheduled for the following Monday, taking it very close to the date for the final itself, which was to be played on the subsequent Saturday.

The second semi-final, between Celtic and Hearts due two nights later, was also a victim of the winter weather, with the Scottish League confirming that the competition would now be put back until late February as it was impractical to play a final just a few days after the semi-finals. Wallace gave the league his full-backing. 'Matches played in these current conditions are almost always a lottery,' he stated. 'The league has made a good decision.' As a bonus, it meant the suspended Tom Forsyth would no longer miss the closing stages of the tournament, strengthening the Ibrox chances of lifting the silverware.

November had seen a red-hot Rangers roar clear at the summit of the Premier Division, but it ended in winter's icy grip. Rangers would next be in action at the weekend when they visited Kilbowie Park, Clydebank, for the first time on league business. They would look to start December as they finished the previous month.

6

December: An Unhappy Christmas

WITH THE League Cup now in cold storage, Rangers only had five scheduled league games to play during the new month. The first of these was at a Kilbowie Park in Clydebank that had seen its previous match against Celtic abandoned at half-time due to the treacherous surface. With the icy weather showing no signs of easing, a postponement looked inevitable all week. That ultimately happened on Friday, 2 December, when the day before the match was due a pitch inspection quickly concluded that the surface was unplayable. Only one fixture survived the freeze in the Premier Division, and Aberdeen took advantage of their rivals having a day off by beating Motherwell at Pittodrie to close the gap at the top back to three points.

Initial talk was to try to reschedule the match in the following midweek, but with the forecast predicting frozen temperatures for a few more days Rangers had to accept the fact they would now be idle until at least the next weekend, when they were due a visit from Jim McLean's talented young Dundee United side.

A long-awaited thaw in the weather started in the midweek, allowing Jock Wallace to reveal to the press on the Thursday that the Ibrox pitch was now perfectly playable, and that he would be naming another unchanged 11. This would be the last match of Tom Forsyth's suspension, with Wallace also confirming that his key defender was now back in full training after his leg injury.

Rangers v Dundee United
Saturday, 10 December 1977, Ibrox
Stewart Kennedy, Sandy Jardine, Alex Miller, John Greig, Colin Jackson, Alex MacDonald, Tommy McLean, Bobby Russell, Derek Johnstone, Gordon Smith, Davie Cooper
Substitutes: Derek Parlane, Bobby McKean

A crowd of 25,000 braved the winter cold, hoping to see Rangers continue where they left off before the unwanted break. And they got the ideal start as the Taysiders were overrun in the opening minutes. It was wave after wave of attack towards goalkeeper Hamish McAlpine right from kick-off, and the pressure took just three minutes to tell. There was a hint of controversy about the goal, however, as Derek Johnstone appeared to impede defender Paul Hegarty before the ball fell to Tommy McLean, the little winger confidently beating McAlpine. Referee Douglas Ramsay saw no infringement and the goal stood, much to the disbelief of the United defenders.

There might have been some luck attached to the goal, but there was no doubt Rangers deserved their lead. Ramsay might have been levelling things up when he refused a clear penalty claim after McAlpine brought down Derek Johnstone inside the area, but he awarded a free kick outside the box while booking the goalkeeper. The Rangers support

DECEMBER: AN UNHAPPY CHRISTMAS

enjoyed a stress-free opening 25 minutes, but there were worried looks all around when McLean had to be carried from the pitch after 26 minutes after a collision with full-back Frank Kopel resulted in the goalscorer receiving a serious looking gash on his leg. Another talented winger, Bobby McKean, was his replacement.

Before half-time, United almost snatched an equaliser out of nowhere. Defender David Narey unleashed a thunderous shot from fully 30 yards that rattled Stewart Kennedy's crossbar, and would have been a goal of the season candidate had it been six inches lower. It would have been a travesty if the teams had left the pitch with the scores level, but it showed how precarious a one-goal lead could be, no matter how one-sided the match.

In the second half Rangers suffered a second injury blow when centre-half Colin Jackson limped off the field, which meant a reshuffle involving Johnstone moving back into the defence and the introduction of Derek Parlane as the attacking spearhead. This didn't seem to alter the flow of the match, and Parlane was involved in the clinching goal. After 67 minutes Gordon Smith took a Parlane pass and finished cleverly for his first goal since late October. His celebration showed just how happy and relieved he was to end this mini drought after such an incredible scoring start to his Ibrox career.

Parlane was desperately unlucky not to make it 3-0 before the end, that same crossbar denying him the goal his play had deserved. The final whistle was greeted by warm applause and cheers from the Ibrox faithful, a thoroughly deserved win keeping their favourites motoring along nicely at the top of the table. Aberdeen also beat St Mirren, meaning the gap remained at three points with Rangers having the advantage of having played one game fewer.

Celtic fans, meanwhile, were starting to fear their grip on the championship was already loose, their recent winning run making no impression on the nine-point chasm to the impressive leaders.

The only worry for Rangers was the injuries to McLean and Jackson, but the manager seemed confident that both men would be back sooner rather than later when quizzed by reporters afterwards. Wallace also would have Forsyth available again, which would be timely should Jackson fail to recover. The next fixture was another home match, with opponents Motherwell looking in some disarray after the resignation of their manager Willie McLean and no successor yet appointed.

By Wednesday, Jackson was back in training and declared fit for the weekend. McLean's injury was more serious, however, needing ten stitches in his leg wound, and on the Friday he was ruled out of the Motherwell match. By then Rangers knew when their postponed League Cup semi-final with Forfar would take place, with the tie now scheduled for Monday, 27 February and the final on Saturday, 18 March should the minnows fail to cause the biggest cup upset since Berwick.

With both Aberdeen and Celtic having tricky-looking away matches, the Rangers fans were hopeful they might extend their lead even further before the usual hectic festive schedule. The 20,000 who avoided Christmas shopping to go along to Ibrox would get their wish.

Rangers v Motherwell
Saturday, 17 December 1977, Ibrox
Stewart Kennedy, Sandy Jardine, John Greig, Tom Forsyth, Colin Jackson, Alex MacDonald, Bobby McKean, Bobby Russell, Derek Johnstone, Gordon

DECEMBER: AN UNHAPPY CHRISTMAS

Smith, Davie Cooper
Substitutes: Alex Miller, Derek Parlane

Tom Forsyth came straight back into the team after his enforced absence, and he was at the centre of some controversy when Rangers eventually took the lead after 25 minutes. Referee George Smith was happy Forsyth won the ball in a crunching tackle on Motherwell's Vic Davidson, a decision that the visiting players disagreed with. Rangers swept upfield, and Davie Cooper hit a shot that beat goalkeeper Stuart Rennie but struck the post. Unluckily for Rennie, the rebound fell to the feet of Gordon Smith, who couldn't miss the unguarded net.

The goal had come at a good time, just as Motherwell's tactic of packing the midfield was starting to frustrate the Rangers crowd and players. It didn't change the Steelmen's attitude, though, with the remainder of the half following the same pattern of Rangers forcing the play but finding gaps in the Motherwell wall hard to find. It would take another goal before the visitors would look to get forward, and it arrived just a few minutes into the second half. It was a brilliant solo effort by Johnstone, the big striker controlling a Cooper pass on the turn before smashing an unstoppable shot high past Rennie from 20 yards to show he was far more than just a threat with his head.

Motherwell now had just 40 minutes to score twice, which seemed unlikely given their lack of threat up until that point. But they gave themselves hope with 15 minutes remaining when Willie Pettigrew set up Peter Miller to shoot low past Kennedy. Their comeback never looked likely to succeed, however, as Rangers dominated the closing stages and regained their two-goal advantage ten minutes later. The scorer was again Gordon Smith, who knocked it home from close range after a fine cross by Bobby McKean.

It was a routine and fully deserved win, the 3-1 scoreline perhaps flattering Motherwell somewhat. And the league table that night made for happy reading for all at Ibrox. Aberdeen lost at Easter Road, meaning Jock Wallace's men now had a commanding five-point lead at the top with a game in hand at the halfway stage of the season. Celtic had also dropped points in a 3-3 draw at St Mirren, meaning the gap between the Old Firm was now into double figures. With a Christmas Eve trip north to Pittodrie just seven days away, many felt that a Rangers win would all but seal the title before 1978 had even arrived.

Tommy McLean had the stitches removed from his leg in time to resume full training by the middle of the week, Wallace in no doubt that the winger would return to the team if he proved his fitness. Meanwhile, Aberdeen boss Billy McNeill told the press that he would be without his recent signing Gordon Strachan because of injury. With Rangers in fine form, and with Smith and Johnstone the two top goalscorers in the Premier Division, most pundits were predicting an away win. Wallace did try to add a note of caution by pointing out that his team had already lost twice at Aberdeen in the season, and that they were too good a team for any Ibrox complacency to set in. His words were to be prophetic.

Aberdeen v Rangers
Saturday, 24 December 1977, Pittodrie
Stewart Kennedy, Sandy Jardine, John Greig, Tom Forsyth, Colin Jackson, Alex MacDonald, Tommy McLean, Bobby Russell, Derek Johnstone, Gordon Smith, Davie Cooper
Substitutes: Bobby McKean, Derek Parlane
The 21,000 inside Pittodrie gave both teams a rousing reception when they took the field, the match feeling more

DECEMBER: AN UNHAPPY CHRISTMAS

like a big cup tie than a routine league match. Despite the difficulties in travelling so far north on Christmas Eve, there was a huge Rangers following, who perhaps saw the match as a chance for the earliest title party in years. But it was soon obvious that the home team had no intention of going down quietly.

Within a couple of minutes of referee John Paterson starting proceedings, Kennedy's goal had survived two close shaves. First, midfielder John McMaster then full-back Stuart Kennedy missed the target by inches with fierce attempts. Kennedy then pulled off an excellent save to deny McMaster, before Rangers finally showed some attacking threat of their own when a Bobby Russell effort forced Bobby Clark into a diving stop. Rangers were gradually weathering the early storm and starting to play some good football, and in 25 minutes Cooper came close to opening the scoring when his thundering drive scraped the post.

It was end-to-end stuff, and on the half hour it was the home fans celebrating when Aberdeen grabbed the crucial first goal. Drew Jarvie and Joe Harper combined to release Ian Gibson, and he calmly slotted the ball past the advancing Kennedy before being swamped by celebrating team-mates. The goal gave the Dons added belief, and they then dominated the remainder of the half. The Rangers defence was being severely tested and just three minutes before the interval they buckled. Harper was again the provider, this time setting up veteran Davie Robb to thump the ball into the net. The men in red received a huge ovation at half-time, with the Rangers fans stunned after watching their table-topping team a distinct second best.

The visitors knew they needed a big start to the second period, but were twice denied by crucial last-gasp tackles from young defender Willie Miller when a goal looked on. Parlane was sent on to replace Smith halfway through the second half as Rangers' need for a goal became more desperate, and the substitute came close with his first touch of the ball. But any hopes of a late comeback ended on 76 minutes when Harper got the goal his overall play had deserved.

At 3-0 Rangers knew the game was lost, and tempers frayed somewhat when some Aberdeen players tried to showboat. Not recommended when John Greig and Alex MacDonald are the closest opposition players! This riled the Rangers support too, and there was a brief interruption to the play with ten minutes left when a small number of fans spilled out on to the edge of the playing surface. Order was quickly restored, and a final dose of salt was rubbed into the wounds in the closing minutes when Jarvie smashed an unstoppable shot into the net from fully 20 yards.

There was still time for Kennedy to pull off a superb save from Harper, before Rangers were denied a last-minute consolation when Clark produced an even more spectacular save to keep out a McLean free kick. The match ended 4-0, the worst defeat Rangers had suffered in the league for 11 years, and a scoreline guaranteed to spoil the Christmas turkey in many households. Jock Wallace was philosophical in defeat, saying, 'We have no excuses. It's now all about the next game against Hibs. It is never easy to take defeat. But if any of my players had ideas that the race for the championship was almost over, the defeat should have taken that thought out of their minds.'

Unlike down south, the Premier Division had no special festive fixture schedule, so it would be a week until that clash with Hibs. The Easter Road team had recovered from a poor spell of results and had enjoyed much better recent form, and Wallace remembered only too well the last time they visited

DECEMBER: AN UNHAPPY CHRISTMAS

Ibrox. It would be the first of three tough-looking fixtures for Rangers, with a trip to Partick followed by the third Old Firm league encounter in the opening week of 1978.

Rangers v Hibs
Saturday, 31 December 1977, Ibrox
Stewart Kennedy, Sandy Jardine, John Greig, Tom Forsyth, Colin Jackson, Alex MacDonald, Tommy McLean, Bobby Russell, Derek Johnstone, Gordon Smith, Davie Cooper
Substitutes: Alex Miller, Derek Parlane

Jock Wallace gave a vote of confidence to the same 11 players who had been so comprehensively beaten at Aberdeen, the only change being Alex Miller on the substitutes' bench. A healthy attendance of over 27,000 started their new year weekend on the Ibrox terraces, as the fans also seemed to have forgiven their heroes for the dismal result in the north.

As at Easter Road earlier in the season, Hibs wore a strange outfit of bright yellow shirts, white shorts and green socks, making it an unusual spectacle for a match between two clubs with such well-known colours that didn't clash.

The first impressive forward run was made by birthday boy Sandy Jardine, the now 29-year-old overlapping well to send in a dangerous cross that just eluded Smith. But as time went by, Rangers started to look increasingly bereft of ideas on how to break down a stubborn and defensive Edinburgh side, who had centre-half George Stewart in especially impressive form.

As more Rangers moves broke down, the visitors started to grow in belief, and they had the next decent chance when Willie Murray was denied by a Kennedy save. It was looking increasingly as if it would take a moment of inspiration to break down the Hibs defence, and Russell almost provided it on 35 minutes when he unleashed a thumping drive from long range that scraped the crossbar.

Both goalkeepers made relatively comfortable saves in the closing stages of the half, Mike McDonald holding a Smith effort and Kennedy denying Ally McLeod's low shot. It wasn't the most entertaining opening 45, a few grumblings of discontent being heard when referee Bill Anderson called a halt.

The second half was a virtual copy of the first with Rangers struggling to create chances against a well-drilled and determined Hibs, and the visitors occasionally threatening when they broke forward. Gordon was perhaps the player who looked most likely to find a goal, and he was unlucky with a 20-yarder that flew just too high with McDonald beaten. But it was Hibs striker Bobby Hutchinson who had the best chance of the early stages, dispossessing Colin Jackson but then inexplicably deciding to try a shot when he had a team-mate unmarked inside him.

The big chance of the match came with under 20 minutes left. McDonald dropped a cross ball at the feet of Cooper just a few yards out, but the winger failed to connect cleanly with the ball allowing Stewart to clear off the line. The Rangers fans were growing unhappier by the minute, and their mood darkened when their striking hero Johnstone was taken off and replaced by Parlane. There was time for one last chance, and it fell to Smith. His shot looked a scorer until McDonald threw himself full-length to make an outstanding save. It was a save that won his team a point, the game then petering out as a 0-0 stalemate.

A Rangers team who had looked well clear at the top and full of goals and confidence just a week before had ended the year on a low. No goals and just one point from the past two matches saw their lead at the top cut to just two points, albeit with a game in hand. Aberdeen now looked the only realistic challengers, as Celtic ended their 1977 miserably too, slumping to defeat against Ayr United for the second time in the season and sitting a massive nine points behind their great adversaries. It looked like a straight race between those two familiar old rivals for the title, captain John Greig and manager Billy McNeill going head-to-head for the biggest prize in Scottish football. The fixtures straight after the turn of the year could be crucial in deciding who would be smiling come May.

7

January: Old Firm Mayhem

ALTHOUGH CELTIC looked too far behind to be realistic title contenders, many Rangers fans still saw the upcoming Old Firm clash as pivotal in the league race. But Rangers had another tough fixture before they could think about the challenge of overcoming their bitter rivals, a trip to Firhill just 48 hours after the disappointment of the Hibs match.

Jock Wallace was dealt a blow in his preparations for the game, with John Greig ruled out by a foot injury, meaning the ever-reliable Alex Miller would again return to the starting 11.

Bertie Auld's Thistle had recently slipped after a great run had seem them sit second in the table a few weeks earlier, but they were still hugely difficult opponents, especially at a time when Rangers seemed short of confidence and short on goals.

Partick Thistle v Rangers
Monday, 2 January 1978, Firhill
Stewart Kennedy, Sandy Jardine, Alex Miller, Tom Forsyth, Colin Jackson, Alex MacDonald, Tommy

JANUARY: OLD FIRM MAYHEM

McLean, Bobby Russell, Derek Johnstone, Gordon Smith, Davie Cooper
Substitutes: Bobby McKean, Derek Parlane

The Glasgow derby attracted a bumper holiday Monday crowd, with almost 28,500 packed into Firhill on a cold and wet afternoon. The fans were treated to a typical derby in the first half, players from both sides fully committed on a muddy surface. Thistle's defence was particularly impressive, full-back Brian Whittaker winning several important challenges. Behind him was Alan Rough, and he also impressed by dealing confidently with everything that was thrown at him.

Rangers looked the better team but the game remained goalless at half-time, meaning it was now 230 minutes since the supporters had last seen their team score. It would only take another ten minutes, however, for that drought to be broken. Predictably, the man who found the net was Derek Johnstone, turning the ball past Rough from ten yards despite the close attention of several defenders. The celebrations were a combination of joy and relief both on and off the pitch.

But that joy didn't last too long as in the 69th minute, slackness in the heart of the Rangers defence allowed big forward Sandy Frame to nip in and equalise. The visiting fans could see the prospect of more dropped points, and it would take a moment of controversy to turn the match back in Rangers' favour. Just six minutes after being pegged back, a good move ended with Gordon Smith firing in a shot that beat Rough but rebounded off the underside of the crossbar. In an incident reminiscent of the 1966 World Cup Final, the ball bounced down before being cleared, but the linesman signalled it had crossed the line and it was a goal. Thistle protested fiercely, but referee Brian McGinlay took the word of his assistant and Rangers were back in front.

In truth, it was an incident that was viewed very much depending on what team you supported. Rangers fans would swear they saw the ball bounce well behind the line, Thistle supporters equally adamant that the ball stayed out and the decision was an injustice. In the days before multiple television angles and goal-line technology, it is an argument never likely to be definitively settled. But the one deniable fact is that a goal was given, and Rangers won the match by 2-1.

With Aberdeen also winning again, the gap at the top was unchanged. But news filtered through from Parkhead that Motherwell had won 1-0 under their new manager, the former Rangers player Roger Hynd. It was now an 11-point chasm between the Old Firm, and Celtic were playing as much for pride as silverware when they would arrive at Ibrox the following Saturday.

In the midweek before the Old Firm clash, Aberdeen showed their determination to maintain their title assault by paying £20,000 to Clyde for highly rated young striker Steve Archibald. Meanwhile, John Greig was winning his fitness battle to lead out his team against Celtic, giving Rangers a timely boost. The captain spoke to reporters on the eve of the match, and when asked about the massive points gap between the teams he replied, 'Of course we are confident we can win, but forget about current form … there is so much pride in this fixture that nothing can be taken for granted.'

His thoughts were echoed by the manager, Wallace stating, 'No matter the league positions this is a game on its own. It's a unique fixture, the best club match in the world. And it will stay that way until the end of time.' Both men were saying the right things, but it didn't stop those in blue who flocked to Ibrox being supremely confident of victory.

Rangers v Celtic

Saturday, 7 January 1978, Ibrox
Stewart Kennedy, Sandy Jardine, John Greig, Tom Forsyth, Colin Jackson, Alex MacDonald, Tommy McLean, Bobby Russell, Derek Johnstone, Gordon Smith, Davie Cooper
Substitutes: Alex Miller, Derek Parlane

Despite their recent woes, there was still a healthy Celtic support in the 55,000 crowd for the 1pm kick-off. When referee John Gordon started the match, it was the underdogs who settled first and created the first chance in the fifth minute, Roy Aitken's shot forcing a good save from Stewart Kennedy. Rangers looked off the pace and they were fortunate not to go behind a few minutes later when Jóhannes Eðvaldsson, scorer twice in the last Ibrox match between the teams, headed straight at Kennedy with the goal at his mercy.

It took over 20 minutes for Rangers to have a worthwhile shot at goal, and a further ten minutes before they won their first corner. But by the half hour the league leaders had gradually started to get more control in midfield, and in the 35th minute they showed their rivals how to take a chance. Bobby Russell slid a fine pass into the path of Gordon Smith, who was running into the Celtic penalty area on the right-hand side, and the former Kilmarnock man struck a blistering shot past the advancing Peter Latchford and into the Celtic net to send the majority of fans inside the stadium into orbit.

Within two minutes of the opener the match descended into total mayhem, and at the centre of the storm was the referee. In Celtic's next attack, Joe Craig looked like getting on the end of a Paul Wilson cross but fell to the ground when challenged by Colin Jackson. The visiting players and fans howled for a penalty, and they thought for a moment their wish had been granted when some misinterpreted Gordon pointing for a goal kick as him pointing to the penalty spot. When they realised their mistake, the official was surrounded by irate Celtic players. Seeing this, the Rangers players took the goal kick quickly and Greig then Davie Cooper played the ball upfield, with Celtic only having two players in their own half while the rest were still chasing after Gordon.

By the time the arguing posse saw what was going on, they were all left well behind as Alex MacDonald and four team-mates went in on the Celtic goal, with just defender Frank Munro and Latchford in their way. MacDonald played the ball across the area to Tommy McLean, who then set up Russell to shoot after drawing Latchford. Russell mishit his shot, allowing Munro to block, but there was captain Greig running in to knock the ball into the empty net.

The emotions at either end of the ground could hardly have been different. The Rangers fans were in joyful celebration, while Celtic's followers, players and officials were incandescent. Off the pitch, some visiting supporters spilled on to the running track and bottles were thrown, with the police required to remove the offenders. On the pitch, the Celtic players refused to restart the match while pointing furiously in the face of the referee, and it took an intervention from trainer Neil Mochan in the centre circle to persuade his players to continue the match. Poor Gordon was a man in the crossfire from that moment on, Celtic convinced he had prevented a 2-0 scoreline from being 1-1 and Rangers fans thinking he was far too lenient in allowing the level of dissent from the Hoops players without any consequences for the players involved.

There were no further contentious moments before half-time, which was probably just as well for all concerned.

JANUARY: OLD FIRM MAYHEM

Still, a 2-0 lead in an Old Firm match where the opposition had been the better team for most of the half was a very satisfactory position for the Ibrox team.

The second half saw Rangers seemingly content to soak up pressure and hit on the break, and both teams had their moments in the first 15 minutes. Then came another moment of controversy, when an Aitken effort beat Kennedy but was cleared on the line by MacDonald. Celtic arms were in the air claiming another penalty, convinced the Rangers midfielder had prevented a goal by using his arm. Gordon waved away their appeals, but there wasn't time for Celtic's anger to ferment as a minute later they pulled a goal back. A free kick was punted high into the Rangers area and knocked down to the feet of Eðvaldsson, who scooped it home from six yards.

There is no room for neutrals in an Old Firm cauldron, but if there were any inside Ibrox they would probably have said it was a goal that Celtic deserved on the balance of play. And just four minutes later it was very nearly 2-2 when Aitken beat Kennedy with a fine shot only to see it come back off the post. Wallace had seen enough and he brought on Derek Parlane for Cooper, with Derek Johnstone then dropping back into a midfield role. This seemed to give Rangers a balance they had lacked, and in the closing stages they took control.

Alex Miller came on for the limping Tommy McLean with eight minutes to play, and six minutes later he was involved in the clinching goal. His quick throw-in sent Sandy Jardine in on goal, and although Latchford parried the full-back's effort, there was the other substitute Parlane on the spot to knock in the rebound from a few yards out. At 3-1 with just seconds to play, the game was up for Celtic, who despite their valiant efforts were now staring at a third successive league defeat, a 13-point deficit behind Rangers, and the unbelievable position of being only one point above the relegation placings.

It turned out to be a very good afternoon for Rangers, as Aberdeen were held to a surprise draw at lowly Ayr. There was also news of the draw for the third round of the Scottish Cup, which was held at Fir Park after the Motherwell v St Mirren encounter. It was a draw made for the newspaper headline writers, with Rangers coming out of the hat to play away to Berwick Rangers, the match to be played on 28 January which would be exactly 11 years since the most famous Scottish Cup giant-killing of them all. It also meant a switch in roles for Jock Wallace, the Ibrox boss having been the goalkeeping player-manager of the minnows on the day they shook Scottish football and altered the course of Rangers' history.

After the exertions of the new year schedule and such a draining Old Firm encounter, Rangers then had the luxury of a week's break before they were due to next play St Mirren at Love Street. Most of the week was taken up by a dispute between Rangers and Berwick on the ticketing arrangements for their upcoming cup tie. General manager Willie Waddell visited the lower-league ground and declared himself so unhappy with the safety arrangements that he decided Rangers would not accept any tickets for the game. His big worry was unsafe terracings and easy access to the ground for ticketless supporters, which he felt made the police decision to allow a crowd limit of 15,000 an unwise and unsafe move. Berwick responded, manager and ex-Ibrox hero Dave Smith saying that the ground was good enough for Wallace in 1967 and so it should be good enough now. Waddell raised the possibility of playing the game at Ibrox, but neither Berwick nor the SFA supported this suggestion. Rangers then decided to write to the SFA requesting they carry out a ground safety inspection before tickets went on sale.

Meanwhile, the latest meeting of the SFA disciplinary committee decided on a four-day suspension for Tommy McLean for his sending off in November against St Mirren at Ibrox, with his boxing opponent from the match, Bobby Reid of St Mirren, escaping a ban completely. This meant McLean would miss the game between the teams on Saturday, but Reid was free to take part. This wasn't a decision that went down well within Ibrox.

As for the match itself, snow all over Scotland in midweek cast doubt on many fixtures, but a Friday thaw and hardworking ground staff in Paisley combined to give the fixture the go-ahead. Wallace took the easy decision to bring in the ex-St Mirren winger Bobby McKean for the unavailable McLean, giving the remainder of the team who had defeated Celtic a vote of confidence.

St Mirren v Rangers
Saturday, 14 January 1978, Love Street
Stewart Kennedy, Sandy Jardine, John Greig, Tom Forsyth, Colin Jackson, Alex MacDonald, Bobby McKean, Bobby Russell, Derek Johnstone, Gordon Smith, Davie Cooper
Substitutes: Alex Miller, Derek Parlane

After some unsavoury scenes at the first Love Street meeting, this match had a restricted all-ticket capacity of 20,000. On a cold but dry afternoon, the Rangers fans saw their team in confident mood right from the first whistle.

The opening 20 minutes were played mostly towards the St Mirren goal, without former Ibrox goalkeeper Donald Hunter being overly troubled. With the Rangers defenders looking in a mood to take no prisoners, and Tom Forsyth in particular winning tackles impressively, Saints struggled to get close to Stewart Kennedy. Then in the 20th minute, the deadly Rangers strike force combined to open the scoring. Gordon Smith did well to make space for himself on the left wing and fire in a low cross and there was Johnstone 12 yards out to flick a delightful finish into the far corner.

The home team responded well with strikers Frank McGarvey and Bobby Torrance both seeing Kennedy deny them. But Rangers looked the more composed team, Russell continuing his impressive debut season with a display full of poise and purpose. There was no further scoring in the first 45 minutes, the scoreline a fair reflection on an entertaining half.

The second half saw much of the same. Russell and Smith were always a threat and the most accomplished players on view, but the home team carried a threat with their pace and enthusiasm, always keeping the experienced Rangers back four on their toes. It felt like one more Rangers goal would kill the contest, and it arrived with 17 minutes to play.

It was yet another assist for summer signing Davie Cooper, and yet another goal for his fellow Ibrox arrival Gordon Smith. Rangers won a free kick right on the St Mirren byline wide on the right. Cooper's beautifully flighted delivery was met at the near post by the head of Smith, and his header had too much power for Hunter to stop it crossing the line. To St Mirren's credit, they continued to press for a consolation goal, but Kennedy was in fine form and was equal to anything that he had to deal with.

It was an impressive win on the road, all the more important as Aberdeen had beaten Celtic at Pittodrie to stay tucked in three points behind. The Parkhead men were now in total disarray, with the word 'relegation' being mentioned even if not seen as a realistic outcome.

With another week before the team played again, there were still plenty of other stories to interest Rangers supporters. First, on Sunday the draw was made for the World Cup in Argentina, with Scotland the only home nation to have qualified. When they were drawn alongside Holland, Peru and Iran in Group 4, confidence levels went through the roof. A typical response came from team captain Bruce Rioch, who declared, 'We play Peru and Iran first, so we should be through before we play Holland.' History would not be kind to Rioch's remarks.

The next day, the Berwick Rangers ticket disagreement rumbled on. The SFA ordered the match to take place at Berwick as drawn after an inspection of the ground, but they did recommend a lower capacity than originally decided, reducing it to 10,500. Willie Waddell was unimpressed, saying Rangers would refuse any tickets and asked fans not to travel over the border. Dave Smith was seen delivering 2,000 tickets for Rangers to the front door at Ibrox, but he had wasted a journey as Waddell returned them to the lower-league side the next day.

Then later that evening, it was reported that Rangers defender Alex Miller had been admitted to hospital with internal bleeding. He was to be kept in for observation and said to be 'comfortable'. This came as a huge surprise; the player had been an unused substitute at Love Street two days earlier. It was initially unclear how serious his illness was, or how long he would miss competitive football.

As Miller was treated, then released from hospital, attention turned to the weekend clash against Ayr United at Ibrox, with Jock Wallace keen to see his team continue on their recent winning ways. A victory looked almost certain with the Ayrshire team struggling to avoid relegation. But the game was thrown into doubt on the Thursday when Scotland woke up to heavy snow, and with a forecast of freezing temperatures for several days few thought the fixture would survive.

By then the row with Berwick seemed to have become immaterial, as they announced that the tie was a complete sell-out, with the 2,000 returned tickets mostly snapped up by Rangers Supporters Clubs determined their members would see their team. This would now be Rangers' next fixture, as the Ayr game was predictably called off on the Friday afternoon after a pitch inspection of the snow-covered Ibrox surface. Wallace immediately decided to give his team the chance to train and relax in warmer surroundings, the first-team squad flying out to Majorca for a few days to take advantage of the enforced winter break. Among the travelling party was midfielder Johnny Hamilton, who had asked for a transfer, unhappy at being unable to regain a first-team spot due to the form of Russell.

After three days in Magaluf the squad returned to chilly Glasgow, with frost still threatening upcoming games in the area. The cup tie at Berwick looked certain to go ahead, though, and predictably the papers were full of stories in the preceding days about the infamous match in 1967 when Wallace as Berwick player-manager inspired his troops to the biggest humiliation in Rangers' history. The goalscorer from that day 11 years previously, Sammy Reid, was on television, radio and in all the papers as the Ibrox fans who had spent years trying to forget about it were forced to relive their nightmare.

Wallace wasn't the only link to that game still at the clubs, of course. John Greig was the skipper of the beaten Rangers team, with Berwick boss Dave Smith a team-mate.

The day finally dawned on Rangers having the chance to right an ancient wrong, and Wallace showed he wasn't willing to take any risks by naming the strongest team he could. Miller was still recovering from his recent health scare, but otherwise Berwick would need to face the men who had put the Ibrox club in a great position to reclaim the Scottish title.

Berwick Rangers v Rangers
Saturday, 28 January 1978, Shielfield Park
Stewart Kennedy, Sandy Jardine, John Greig, Tom Forsyth, Colin Jackson, Alex MacDonald, Tommy McLean, Bobby Russell, Derek Johnstone, Gordon Smith, Davie Cooper
Substitutes: Derek Parlane, Ally Dawson

John Greig was given an even bigger welcome than usual on to the pitch, as on the eve of the game Rangers confirmed that their long-serving captain would be given the honour of a testimonial match towards the end of the season, the first player to be awarded a benefit fixture since another great captain, Davie Meiklejohn, back in the days between the wars. The game would be between Rangers and a Scotland team managed by national team boss Ally McLeod, and would be sure to attract a huge crowd to Ibrox in April.

There was a carnival atmosphere among the home fans, with one banner laughingly proclaiming 'Jock Wallace is a Traitor'! But once the serious action started, the wee Rangers almost gave their famous visitors the worst start possible. With less than 20 seconds on the clock winger Ian Smith burst clear down the right, and his low cross flashed across the Rangers goal, beating the stranded Kennedy but also just eluding Eric Tait as he ran in on goal. It would signal the start of an afternoon that goalkeeper Kennedy would want to forget.

The underdogs continued to take the fight to the overwhelming favourites, but after ten minutes some reality was restored. Tommy McLean flighted in a corner, and there was centre-half Colin Jackson rising highest to nod the ball past goalkeeper John Lyle. It was exactly what Rangers had needed, the goal dampening the rising spirits of the home crowd, who must have thought their team had to score first to have any chance.

This dominance in the air was to prove to be the decisive factor on the day, as the second goal arrived some 27 minutes later and looked very familiar. Another McLean corner, another towering Jackson header, another ball well beyond Lyle.

The big, unapproved travelling support surely now could relax, with the 2-0 half-time scoreline meaning the job was done.

It should have been but Kennedy had a nightmare second half, and he handed Berwick a lifeline 13 minutes after the interval with a real clanger. The big goalkeeper, whose mistakes at Wembley in a 5-1 defeat to England had ended his promising international career, had been in good form in recent matches. But he was badly at fault when dropping a harmless cross straight at the feet of Ian Smith, who couldn't believe his luck as he rolled the ball into the empty Rangers net.

The home fans were awake again, ramping up the noise inside the tiny ground, but their joy only lasted for three minutes. It was Lyle's turn for a goalkeeping howler; a looping Johnstone header should have been a routine save, but the stopper misjudged the flight, assuming it would drift over the bar. He looked on in horror as the ball dropped under the crossbar and into his net, giving Rangers a third headed goal and restoring the two-goal lead.

That seemed to be that, and Rangers looked to see the game out without any further excitement. But Kennedy flapped at another harmless cross ball with four minutes remaining, Gordon Laing the lucky recipient of his gift this time as he sent the Berwick fans wild from all of two yards out. Wallace was stony-faced in the dugout as Kennedy appealed in vain to referee Bill Mullan for a non-existent foul, although Johnstone did his best to calm the boss just a minute later when he scored with yet another header. The match ended 4-2, Berwick leaving the pitch to a heroic reception while the Rangers players must have wondered what their manager was going to say despite them going safely into the next round.

Dave Smith praised the spirit of his players, and pointed out that not too many sides had scored twice against the league leaders. Wallace, meanwhile, remained diplomatic in public, giving the underdogs great credit for pushing his team, and also speaking of his delight for John Greig, the only Rangers player on the pitch who had suffered the ignominy of the 1967 result.

The draw for the next round took place after the match, although it was an uncertain group of ties that it produced after a weekend where only six of the 16 scheduled matches survived the weather. Rangers were given a decent-looking fourth round draw, with their opponents being the winners of the game between Stirling Albion and Clydebank.

A stop-start January drew to a close with Rangers still very much in contention for all three Scottish honours. They were hoping the weather wouldn't disrupt any more fixtures, as they already had a full-looking calendar ahead.

8

February: The Battle of Fir Park

THE FIRST match of the new month was the easiest-looking league fixture possible, at home to a Clydebank side rooted to the bottom of the table. The big question in the week leading up to it was whether it would go ahead after the winter freeze wiped out the rearranged Scottish Cup midweek ties. Luckily, a thaw arrived just in time, and the match went ahead as planned.

Rangers v Clydebank
Saturday, 4 February 1978, Ibrox
Peter McCloy, Sandy Jardine, John Greig, Alex Miller, Colin Jackson, Alex MacDonald, Tommy McLean, Bobby Russell, Derek Johnstone, Gordon Smith, Davie Cooper
Substitutes: Derek Parlane, Bobby McKean

After announcing an unchanged 11 to the press on Friday, Jock Wallace was forced into a late change of mind when goalkeeper Stewart Kennedy reported a foot injury after training, so his long-time rival for the number one jersey, Peter McCloy, returned to the team for the first time since the 3-3 draw at St Mirren in September. There may have

FEBRUARY: THE BATTLE OF FIR PARK

been many in the 17,000 crowd who had assumed that Kennedy was dropped after his mistakes at Berwick, but Wallace was at pains to point out after the match that the change in goalkeeper was entirely due to injury.

There was then further disruption to the expected starting line-up when Tom Forsyth pulled up with a muscle injury during the warm-up, resulting in a last-minute reshuffle which saw the return of the now fully recovered Alex Miller, who was initially listed as a substitute. Bemused fans listened on as the Ibrox tannoy announced minutes before kick-off that both Bobby McKean and Ally Dawson were to report to the main door of the stadium, presumably so one of them could take Miller's place on the bench. McKean became the 13th man, so it could only be assumed that he made it to the meeting place first.

Clydebank started the match a massive nine points adrift at the bottom of the table, with just three league wins from 20 attempts. The conditions may have helped level things out against the leaders, the midweek cold and frost now replaced by driving rain, helping turn the Ibrox pitch quite quickly into something of a mudheap. But despite the conditions the fixture quickly became a contest between the Rangers attack and an inspired Clydebank goalkeeper, Jim Gallacher. He produced saves from each of the five players in the Ibrox forward line in the first half, and threw in another excellent stop from Sandy Jardine for good measure.

The Bankies struggled to get out of their own half in the opening 45 minutes, but somehow went back to the warmth of the away dressing room with their goal intact, Gallacher deserving his ten-minute rest more than anyone. When the teams re-emerged, Rangers had changed into pristine fresh strips while the visitors still wore their mud-splattered outfits from the first half. But the new look did nothing to alter the flow of the game.

Gallacher again was the one-man defensive wall that Rangers couldn't breach. He made a spectacular save from Derek Johnstone, then as time started to tick away he similarly denied substitute Derek Parlane. Going into the closing stages, both substitutes were now on the park, as late call-up McKean was needed after Tommy McLean limped off. There was then a scare for the home fans when in almost their first attack of the game, Clydebank had a great chance to score but Gerry Ronald elected to shoot from an acute angle when he had a player unmarked in the middle.

It was beginning to look like an unexpected and surprising dropped point, then with just eight minutes left Gallacher was finally beaten. Referee Tom Kellock awarded a Rangers free kick out wide. Bobby Russell flighted in a teasing delivery, and there was the deadly Johnstone to break Kilbowie hearts with a powerful and accurate header. It was Rangers' 50th league goal of the season, and few others had been as welcome. The home fans celebrated the late winner, and they were cheered even further after the match when they discovered that Aberdeen had drawn at Motherwell and the lead at the top was now four points.

It was maybe timely that the team had a free midweek now Kennedy, Forsyth and McLean had all picked up injuries. Several other sides were involved in rearranged Scottish Cup ties, and with their players now otherwise occupied, Ally McLeod called up both Bobby Russell and Gordon Smith into the Scotland under-21 team to face Wales at Chester. Among those cup ties the match between Stirling Albion and Clydebank to decide Rangers' next opponents. Unfortunately, the wait to find out who

FEBRUARY: THE BATTLE OF FIR PARK

would play at Ibrox on 18 February went on another 24 hours as the match was abandoned on the Monday night in the second half due to thick fog. The next night it finally got completed, and it was little Stirling Albion who had an Ibrox payday to look forward to after they beat the Premier Division side 3-0.

Russell and Smith both started for the under-21s, but despite the team also containing young talent such as John Wark of Ipswich, Alex McLeish of Aberdeen and Roy Aitken of Celtic, they slumped to a 1-0 loss. There was better news for the three injured Rangers stars, with Wallace declaring that they were all in contention to play in the upcoming Tannadice clash with Dundee United, with Forsyth the one causing most concern. Their fitness looked like turning out to be academic, however, with United's snowbound pitch unplayable in midweek for a game scheduled against Motherwell, and the Tayside weather forecast suggesting an improvement unlikely.

The inevitable postponement took place early on the Saturday morning, with all five Premier Division games falling victim to this latest freeze. There was now a real backlog of outstanding matches, with Rangers having to find rearranged dates for league fixtures with Clydebank, Ayr United and Dundee United, in addition to the delayed completion of the League Cup. They agreed with Ayr United to try to play their game on the following Wednesday night, but the chances of this happening looked bleak according to the Met Office. Despite optimistic noises from Wallace, who went as far as naming a team that contained both Kennedy and McLean but left out Forsyth, the game was called off after a pitch inspection at noon on matchday.

The woes of the Scottish football calendar were briefly relegated to the inside pages of the newspapers at the end of the week, to cover the shock news from America that the great Muhammad Ali had sensationally lost his undisputed world heavyweight title to the relative unknown, Leon Spinks. Time looked to have caught up with the man known as The Greatest, but the Scottish weather was something that could be reversed, and the good news on the Friday was that a few pitches in the west of the country were starting to thaw. This meant plans were made to make the most of any playable surfaces. Rangers were hopeful that Ibrox would get passed fit to stage the visit of Stirling Albion in the cup and also agreed with Clydebank that they would play the previously postponed league game at Kilbowie 24 hours later if weather permitted.

In the event, only three cup ties survived, at Greenock, Dumbarton and Ibrox. Referee David Syme's verdict on the Ibrox surface must have been borderline, as the pitch still was rock-hard in places. The players might not have all agreed with his decision. Kilbowie also got the green light from its inspection, so after a recent famine of football, Rangers fans now looked forward to two matches in the one weekend.

Rangers v Stirling Albion
Saturday, 18 February 1978, Ibrox
Stewart Kennedy, Sandy Jardine, Alex Miller, John Greig, Colin Jackson, Alex MacDonald, Tommy McLean, Bobby Russell, Derek Johnstone, Gordon Smith, Davie Cooper
Substitutes: Derek Parlane, Eric Morris

The optimism over Tom Forsyth's fitness had proved to be misplaced, the big defender being ruled out of both weekend matches. The players took to the field wearing training shoes, no studs would be able to penetrate the surface, and some in the 15,000 crowd may have feared the conditions would prove a great leveller and give the First Division underdogs more of a chance than normal.

Albion did give the home defence a couple of worrying moments early on as the players tried to adjust to the solid surface, but the match soon settled into the predictable pattern of Rangers going forward and the lower-league team packing their defence to frustrate both the Ibrox crowd and players. It was McLean who looked most likely to stay on his feet and fashion the opener, with the little winger twice finding the head of Johnstone in the opening quarter of an hour but visiting goalkeeper George Young denying the prolific striker.

It may have seemed unusual for some of the older Rangers fans in the stadium to be cheering when George Young was beaten, but after 19 minutes the goalkeeper with the legendary Ibrox name was helpless to prevent Johnstone adding to his impressive goals tally. It was a case of third time lucky – another McLean cross, another header, but this time it had the power and direction to find the net.

There may have been over 70 minutes to play, but everyone inside the ground knew the contest had been decided. Sales of Bovril must have been excellent as the small crowd shivered in the Glasgow cold, with the match doing little to keep their circulation flowing. Alex MacDonald came close, but when Syme ended the first half there was still just that solitary Johnstone goal separating the teams. In truth, however, there was also a chasm between the sides in belief, Albion looking happy to survive with pride intact and no injuries to their players.

The second half saw more of the same with the Rangers players looking hesitant on the solid surface, and the visitors frightened to leave any gaps in defence just in case. It was perhaps typical of the day when Sandy Jardine burst forward, seemingly finding some softer ground where he could run at the Stirling back line, only for the Scotland international to slip and crash to the ground. He limped off the pitch, giving the fans a rare glimpse of reserve team regular Eric Morris and handing Wallace a potential injury worry for the league match due 24 hours later. Parlane was also given the final stages, Wallace maybe fearing he would suffer hypothermia by sitting on the bench any longer.

The fans started heading towards the exits long before the end, no doubt seeking the warmth of something stronger than Bovril. Many missed a late scare when the recalled Stewart Kennedy had to defrost himself enough to make a good save from a shot by number four Jim Clark. It was the final action of a match that could be best described as 'instantly forgettable', but Rangers were into the last eight and had a fixture played when most of their rivals were going to have to fit in a midweek match in the near future.

The quarter-final draw was made after one of the other surviving ties at Boghead, where Dumbarton drew with Hearts. With so many matches postponed it threw up no definite ties, but one mouthwatering possibility. Rangers were drawn at home to play the winner of the match between Celtic and Kilmarnock, with the probability of an Old Firm cup tie on 11 March. There was also still the chance the teams could meet in the final of the League Cup, which was due to be played the Saturday after the Scottish Cup quarter-finals. Incredibly, the league fixture due the week after that was Celtic v Rangers at Parkhead. There was now the very real chance of three successive Old Firm Saturdays, at three different venues in three different competitions. The fans' excitement was matched only by the trepidation of the police.

FEBRUARY: THE BATTLE OF FIR PARK

The next afternoon, there were 10,000 fans shivering inside Kilbowie Park as Rangers looked to increase their lead at the top of the league table to six points. They would need to do that without Jardine, however, whose ankle injury suffered the previous day had ruled him out of both this match and the midweek Scotland international friendly against Bulgaria.

The two main talking points as the teams emerged from the tunnel were centred around John Greig and Derek Johnstone. With a Salvation Army band leaving the pitch after providing pre-match music, this gave a reminder of various newspaper headlines which featured quotes from several religious organisations in Scotland condemning Rangers for agreeing to play the upcoming testimonial for their captain on a Sunday. The club had not yet responded to this criticism, although with such fixture congestion it looked difficult to arrange the game for a different day given top players from both sides of the border would be in action.

Johnstone was providing a very different talking point. Sporting a new fashionable permed hairstyle, it prompted terracing jokes on how this trendy new look would interfere with his deadly heading ability. Wallace elected to make just the one change to his starting line-up, with Alex Miller moving across to right-back to replace the injured Jardine, and youngster Ally Dawson given the left-back position.

Clydebank v Rangers
Sunday, 19 February 1978, Kilbowie Park
Stewart Kennedy, Alex Miller, Ally Dawson, John Greig, Colin Jackson, Alex MacDonald, Tommy McLean, Bobby Russell, Derek Johnstone, Gordon Smith, Davie Cooper
Substitutes: Derek Parlane, Eric Morris

Clydebank went into the match rooted at the bottom of the table and already out of the Scottish Cup, seemingly the perfect opponents for Rangers in their mission to extend their championship lead. They were also without their influential defender Jim Fallon, who had played so well in the recent meeting between the teams at Ibrox. The last thing the home fans would have wanted was to concede an early goal. The last thing they wanted then happened.

McLean trotted across to the left wing to take a sixth-minute corner, again wearing training shoes on another bone-hard surface. His cross saw Johnstone, Gordon Smith and goalkeeper Jim Gallacher all leap together, and it was the newly curled head of Johnstone which won the contest as he scored in his fifth successive game. Some fans behind the goal thought Smith may have got the final touch, but DJ was quick to claim it, and his name is the one on the match records.

The early goal settled Rangers, and with Alex MacDonald at his driving best in the engine room, there looked every chance this would be a game Wallace's men could kill off early on. Gallacher did his best to keep his team in it but the pressure told in the 26th minute. There was no doubt this time as to the goalscorer, Johnstone finishing expertly after being sent clear by Smith. The rejigged Rangers defence did have a close shave a few minutes later when Gerry Ronald beat the offside trap but he lobbed the ball over both Kennedy and the crossbar when clean through. This would have been an undeserved lifeline for the Bankies, however, and the half-time score of 2-0 did not flatter the league leaders.

The second half was a much more even contest, albeit Rangers seemed content with their two-goal advantage. Clydebank's Dave Houston and Jim Lumsden both passed

FEBRUARY: THE BATTLE OF FIR PARK

up good chances which might have made for an interesting finale, but Rangers survived this mini onslaught and then tied the points up with 18 minutes left when former Kilbowie hero Davie Cooper headed home from another McLean corner.

When referee Mike Delaney ended the match, the 3-0 scoreline was perhaps slightly rough on Clydebank for their second-half efforts, but overall there could be no complaints at the destination of the points. Wallace summed things up in one short sentence. 'It was a good weekend's work,' he said. The newspaper reports the following day agreed with his sentiments, with some writers now saying the title race was over and Rangers were uncatchable. Wallace brushed aside such suggestions, insisting there were still many hard matches to play, starting with a difficult-looking trip to Motherwell the following weekend, the Fir Park team on a good run of form since the appointment of ex-Rangers defender Roger Hynd as their new manager.

Johnstone was the only Rangers player in the Scotland squad after the withdrawals of injured pair Tom Forsyth and Sandy Jardine, and Wallace decided to reward his squad for their winning weekend by giving the players three days off, with training to resume again on the Thursday morning. Despite his impressive scoring streak, Johnstone was named only as a substitute by Ally McLeod for the Hampden international, coming on for Joe Jordan in the second half in a 2-1 Scotland win.

With efforts elsewhere to get games played all failing, it was announced that the Celtic v Kilmarnock cup tie would be played the following Monday, the same night as Rangers took on Forfar in the League Cup semi-final, and two days before Celtic then played Hearts in the other semi. Hearts also had a rearranged Scottish Cup tie squeezed into their schedule on that same Monday night, as the winter backlog now started to bite teams.

Rangers, meanwhile, were able to prepare for Fir Park, with a capacity crowd expected as Motherwell went into the game on a six-game unbeaten run. Wallace confirmed that Jardine and Forsyth were both making good progress from injury, and he delayed naming a team on the Friday to give both players every chance of making it, saying both would start if confirmed fully fit.

With Rangers riding high at the top and Motherwell's defence having kept six successive clean sheets, few were in doubt that this was the match of the day in Scotland. The weather had now thawed, the pitch was soft and perfectly playable, and a big crowd of over 20,000 created a cup-tie atmosphere inside a packed Fir Park.

Motherwell v Rangers
Saturday, 25 February 1978, Fir Park
Stewart Kennedy, Alex Miller, John Greig, Tom Forsyth, Colin Jackson, Alex MacDonald, Tommy McLean, Bobby Russell, Derek Johnstone, Gordon Smith, Davie Cooper
Substitutes: Derek Parlane, Ally Dawson

Jardine was initially in the team, but then pulled back out after being unable to take part in the warm-up. Forsyth did return, however, meaning youngster Ally Dawson dropped to the bench. The cold and frost had been replaced by driving rain, meaning the covered areas within the ground were bursting at the seams.

Referee Eddie Thomson started a match that began at breakneck speed and then rarely slowed down. Tackles flew in from both sides, with the official being kept busy trying to maintain order. The first chance fell to Motherwell centre-half Willie McVie, when his header from a Peter Marinello corner beat Kennedy only for John Greig to clear off the line. Rangers responded and their first chance was also from a header, predictably a Johnstone effort from a McLean cross. The big striker was off target on this occasion.

Peter Miller was booked for a high tackle on Bobby Russell after 20 minutes as the game continued to ebb and flow. Both teams looked capable of scoring, and five minutes later it was the home fans who celebrated the opener. Marinello curled in a teasing cross that was met by former Hibs man Jim O'Rourke. He sent a floated, accurate header high past Kennedy and into the far corner of the net. A confident Motherwell team now had their tails up and flooded forward, and just three minutes later Rangers were in real trouble. Marinello was again the creator, slipping a perfectly timed pass to Vic Davidson in the inside-left position. Davidson drew Kennedy but saw his initial shot blocked. Unfortunately for the Rangers stopper the ball then looped into the air, allowing Davidson to nod the rebound home.

As the Motherwell players and fans celebrated, there were ugly scenes in the covered enclosure opposite the main stand as angry Rangers fans started spilling on to the playing surface and bottles and other missiles were thrown. Stories emerged after the game of the support reacting to an offensive gesture by a Motherwell player towards them, and although this was never confirmed by television pictures, it was seemingly confirmed by several eye witnesses inside the ground. Whatever the reason, hundreds of Rangers supporters swarmed on to the pitch, forcing Thomson to take the players off the field for around four minutes while police tried to remove the offenders and restore calm. Several arrests were made before team captains John Greig and Joe Wark were able to lead their teams back out of the tunnel.

Rangers restarted the match two goals down against a rampant Motherwell. But this team had resilience to match their undoubted ability, and they refused to buckle. Greig was leading the way, his rampaging run from the back ending with a half chance and a huge roar from the Rangers end. All of a sudden it was waves of royal blue attack, and in the 36th minute the score was 2-1. A Smith header sent Johnstone running in on goal. The big man then showed his underrated footballing ability as he cleverly chipped the ball over the advancing Stuart Rennie, ran round the goalkeeper, and then found the net with a diving header.

The anger in the Rangers terraces turned to joy as Motherwell now creaked under immense pressure, and just two minutes later their joy turned to sheer ecstasy. A swift counterattack after Greig cleared a Motherwell free kick saw MacDonald win a crunching tackle wide on the right and break free. He slipped the ball inside to Cooper, who in turn teed up Smith as Rangers poured men forward. Smith showed great composure to pass the ball into the corner of the net from eight yards and an incredible match was now level. There was still time for Rangers to be denied a penalty when Smith appeared to be brought down before the referee brought a breathless first half to an end.

There was no doubt Rangers now had the momentum, with the Motherwell supporters hoping the interval would give their team a chance to regain their composure. But the second period started as the first had ended, Rangers dominant and the Motherwell defence by far the busier. Just four minutes had passed when McLean was scythed down by Wark 25 yards out on the right. The winger picked himself up and took the free kick, his chipped ball finding

FEBRUARY: THE BATTLE OF FIR PARK

the head of Colin Jackson whose effort was blocked. The ball popped up into the air and was then nodded down by Smith to Cooper, and the summer signing gave Rennie no chance with a firm strike from close range.

From 2-0 down to 3-2 up, the tide had now completely turned and Rangers were in the mood to give up their advantage. With Forsyth now looking back up to speed at the back, and Russell orchestrating things in the middle, the league leaders went for the kill. The fourth goal took just eight minutes more to arrive, and it was another classic for the lethal Johnstone. A high clearance saw the centre-forward outjump McVie to head the ball past him and into acres of space. Johnstone then showed great pace to run on to his own flick and bear down on goal. As the goalkeeper came to meet him, the Premier Division's top goalscorer casually clipped it over his body and the ball rolled into the corner of the net. A stunning solo effort, and Johnstone's ninth goal in six matches.

McVie's afternoon got even worse a few minutes later. As a chorus of 'We're going to win the league' rang out from the Rangers fans, McLean's low, hard cross was thundered into his own net by the hapless Motherwell defender as he tried to stop the ball reaching the lurking Johnstone. After six matches without conceding, Motherwell had now seen the ball hit their net an amazing five times in just half an hour of football. To their credit, they kept fighting until the end, and Davidson restored some respectability to the scoreline when he hit his second goal of the afternoon with just over 20 minutes remaining.

Eight goals, a pitch invasion, and an amazing comeback made for a memorable afternoon, with Wallace ecstatic at full time. Although keen to praise his team's mental strength and goalscoring power, he was quick to point out that they had a League Cup semi-final just 48 hours later, and Forfar would be regarded as a similar threat to his team as Motherwell. 'Forfar are in the semi-final on merit,' he said, 'and they will be treated with the respect due to a club who have got there.'

Aberdeen kept up their distant pursuit by beating Hibs, but Celtic's awful league season showed no sign of easing as their home defeat to St Mirren meant they were only out of the relegation places on goal difference. Aberdeen were the visitors to Ibrox in seven days, with a home win surely wrapping up a 37th league title at Ibrox. But such heady thoughts had to wait, with Forfar and their wily player-manager Archie Knox the next obstacle to be overcome.

Forfar Athletic v Rangers
Monday, 27 February 1978, Hampden
Stewart Kennedy, Alex Miller, John Greig, Tom Forsyth, Colin Jackson, Alex MacDonald, Tommy McLean, Bobby Russell, Derek Johnstone, Gordon Smith, Davie Cooper
Substitutes: Derek Parlane, Ally Dawson

It was difficult to believe this was a major cup semi-final, with only 13,000 fans bothering to make the trip to the national stadium on a cold and wet Monday night. Forfar's tiny band of hopefuls could even be heard occasionally as the small Rangers support who did make the effort seemed to be there out of duty rather than excitement. In among some tasty league fixtures, perhaps the thought of a procession against lower-league opponents wasn't enough to get the juices flowing.

It was therefore up to the players to provide the excitement and improve the atmosphere, Wallace having a straightforward task in selecting the exact same 13 from that fabulous contest at the weekend. That task was all the easier with Sandy Jardine ruled out again, with all at the club hopeful the best right-back in the country would be fit again for the Aberdeen showdown in five days. The Forfar team contained a man who had provided Rangers fans with a previous League Cup day to remember – Alex Rae was Partick Thistle's captain when they famously beat Celtic 4-1 in the 1971 final. A win would surely give him the most unlikely, and most incredible, cup double ever.

The match started in as low-key a fashion as the attendance merited, although Rangers took control of possession quickly and were the team pressing forward. Too many passes went astray, however, allowing the eager underdogs to snuff out the danger. The groans from those in blue scarves were just beginning to get more audible when Rangers, wearing their red away shirts, found the breakthrough after 25 minutes. It started with a familiar source, an accurate McLean cross. This time, however, it was Smith at the back post who was on the end of it, and he nodded it back across the six yard line for strike partner Johnstone to head past the despairing dive of Dave Nicholl.

The Ibrox faithful could now relax; surely this was the beginning of a goals avalanche. But the Loons had other ideas and stormed forward in search of a leveller. Dougie Clark had the ball in the Rangers net but had been flagged well offside before knocking it past Stewart Kennedy. Rangers then survived a decent penalty claim when Kenny Payne looked to have been brought down by Forsyth. Wallace's team were holding on grimly for half-time, but they failed to get there. With just a minute before referee Eddie Thomson's watch reached the 45th minute, the Rangers fans were stunned into silence by a deserved equaliser. Ken Brown took possession 25 yards out, and with no defender coming to challenge him, he had time to unleash a deadly accurate shot which beat Kennedy and went in off the post.

When the teams left the pitch seconds later, the Rangers fans let their team know how disappointed they were. That disappointment would soon turn to full-blown panic. After 15 more frustrating minutes of the second half Rangers were awarded a free kick just inside the Forfar half. Jackson and Greig went forward for the expected long ball, but Rangers made an almighty mess of the kick. Forsyth played it short to McLean, expecting to see the winger then look to find the head of a team-mate in the packed Forfar area. But McLean dallied and was dispossessed by Brian Rankin. The left-back then had 60 yards of empty pitch to run into, with McLean frantically trying to get back and Greig racing across the pitch to try to close the space. The Forfar man showed great pace, then great composure as he sped into the Rangers area and scored with a low shot just before Greig could get to him.

Rangers now had half an hour to avoid a result that would match Berwick in 1967 as the most calamitous cup shock in club history. Derek Parlane was thrown on as an extra forward for the closing stages, Cooper making way. But as time went on it started to look as if the underdogs were about to enjoy their greatest night, Rangers wasting any chances falling their way. There were just seven minutes to go when humiliation was avoided. McLean, the man whose mistake led to the Forfar goal, showed the more familiar side to his game. His beautifully flighted cross from the left was met by the head of Parlane and the ball flew low past Nicholl and in off the same post that had guided home Forfar's first-half equaliser.

FEBRUARY: THE BATTLE OF FIR PARK

Parlane was mobbed by his team-mates, whose relief was obvious. The part-timers slumped to the ground, so close to immortality, knowing they were unlikely now to hold off their faster, fitter and more illustrious opponents. They did survive until full time, however, meaning 30 minutes of extra time would be required. Wallace was seen shaking his fists angrily during the on-pitch team talk that followed, the manager clearly not impressed with what he had seen. Extra time was to be the one-sided affair the fans had expected before the match.

Forfar were already hanging on grimly after five extra minutes when McLean took possession and played a clever switch of play to Alex MacDonald. The midfielder ran forward before hitting a magnificent low, swerving shot from 20 yards that left Nicholl helpless, the ball going in off that same post for a third time in the match. 'Doddie' raised an arm aloft and ran to the fans, with his team-mates and those on the terraces all now certain that Rangers were into another cup final. Forfar's legs had gone, the tank was empty, and Rangers were in no mood to ease off. Five minutes later McLean was the man behind their fourth goal. His in-swinging corner from the left deceived Nicholl, allowing Parlane to rise unchallenged at the back post to nod the ball home from almost under the crossbar.

McLean had been involved in all four Rangers goals, as well as the second one for Forfar. And the twinkle-toed winger found yet another assist three minutes into the second half of extra time. He picked the ball up fully 30 yards out and ran straight at the tiring Forfar back line, beating three men before squaring it to Johnstone for an easy finish. The match ended 5-2, a second successive match where Rangers had hit five, but one where the scoreline in no way reflected just how close to disaster they had come.

Despite his obvious displeasure earlier, Wallace chose to praise his team after the match. 'Full marks to my boys,' he growled. 'They were 2-0 down at Motherwell and were behind again tonight. It shows their determination, character and quality.' Rightly, Wallace also took time to compliment his opponents, calling Forfar 'magnificent'. He also added, 'They came out to play football against us, and did exactly that. That has to be good for the game.'

There was little quality on show across the city that night as Celtic stumbled to a 1-1 draw with Kilmarnock in their Scottish Cup tie, meaning a replay would be needed before Rangers knew their quarter-final opponents. Killie, despite being without their 'loan Ranger' Colin Stein due to flu, had been just six minutes away from a famous win. Celtic did improve two nights later, however, seeing off Hearts in the other League Cup semi-final to confirm an Old Firm final on Saturday, 18 March.

Rangers had enjoyed a perfect February, five wins from five games with progress in both cups as well as building a big lead in the league. With Derek Johnstone looking in unstoppable form, and with 15 goals scored in those five games, they headed into spring in great shape.

9

March: Tragedy and Triumph

THE NEW month looked like being a pivotal one for Rangers. In the league they had an upcoming visit from their only realistic challengers, Aberdeen, on the first weekend, plus the final Old Firm clash at Parkhead towards the end of March. There would also be a League Cup Final against the old enemy, as well as a likely Scottish Cup quarter-final at Ibrox to play against them if they finally shook off First Division Kilmarnock. The bookmakers had given odds of just 6/1 on a treble, but any such talk was given short shrift by Jock Wallace, who was determined there would no room for complacency, especially after the near-calamity against Forfar.

All the talk in the media in the build-up to the visit of Aberdeen was of Rangers virtually clinching the title. Even old foe Billy McNeill admitted, 'I accept if Rangers beat us then the championship is sewn up.' This public face was without doubt different from what was being said behind closed doors, with the Dons hitting good form and recent signing Steve Archibald looking to be an excellent goalscoring acquisition.

Wallace received a blow to his plans on the eve of the game when Sandy Jardine failed a fitness test, meaning Alex

Miller continued at right-back and another game went by without the fans seeing the recognised first-choice back four. A big crowd was expected at Ibrox for the virtual crowning of the new champions, but on a day of reasonable weather a slightly disappointing attendance of 34,500 was given as the official figure. Maybe those who decided to stay away had a premonition of what was to come.

Rangers v Aberdeen
Saturday, 4 March 1978, Ibrox
Stewart Kennedy, Alex Miller, John Greig, Tom Forsyth, Colin Jackson, Alex MacDonald, Tommy McLean, Bobby Russell, Derek Johnstone, Gordon Smith, Davie Cooper
Substitutes: Derek Parlane, Ally Dawson

With the prospect of an eight-point mountain to climb if they were defeated, Aberdeen approached the match like a cup final and they quickly took control of the midfield with their high-energy style. Bobby Russell and Alex MacDonald struggled to contain the running of John McMaster, Dom Sullivan and Drew Jarvie, and this resulted in the visiting forwards seeing far more of the ball than in in-form Ibrox attack. Russell in particular looked strangely lethargic after such an impressive debut season, with the Ibrox crowd sensing things were not going well from early on.

Archibald had already come close to beating Stewart Kennedy before he grabbed a deserved opener for the Dons midway through the first half, finishing off a fine move that involved Jarvie and centre-forward Joe Harper. As well as their midfield dominance, Aberdeen were succeeding in nullifying much of Rangers' attacking threat by deploying double marking on Gordon Smith whenever he received the ball, forcing him man to wander into less effective wide areas to try to find space.

Goalkeeper Bobby Clark had little to do, but was called into action briefly when Derek Johnstone found enough room to get in a shot, but the main direction of attacking flow was towards Kennedy. Wallace was probably hoping his team could hold out until the interval and look to alter his tactics, but his hopes were dashed in the 38th minute when Harper pounced on a loose ball to hammer a shot into the Rangers net through the legs of Kennedy. Trailing 2-0 and being badly outplayed, Rangers already looked a beaten team.

Russell didn't reappear after the break; it was later confirmed that he had felt unwell during the first half and had been sick in the dressing room at half-time. This perhaps went some way to explaining the midfield dominance Aberdeen were enjoying. This meant an unfamiliar midfield role in the second half for young full-back Ally Dawson, and although he tried manfully and showed some good touches, he was never able to reverse the momentum that had been built up in the first 45 minutes.

The second period still saw the visitors creating the better openings, and Wallace threw the dice one last time by withdrawing Smith and going with a double centre-forward attack of Derek Parlane alongside Johnstone. This switch was greeted by derision from many on the slopes of Ibrox, and the two Dereks got little change out of centre-backs Willie Garner and Willie Miller. The misery for those in blue was completed with 12 minutes remaining when Archibald scored his second of the afternoon with another clinical finish. And it could have been worse, Archibald missing an easy chance late on that would have completed his hat-trick.

McNeill punched the air when referee Tommy Muirhead ended the Ibrox torture with the score still 3-0, the gap now down to four points and a second successive hammering for Rangers at his team's hands. With ten games still to play the title race was now very much alive again, and some wondered what psychological effect this would have on Rangers after many had assumed they already had the championship in the bag.

Wallace was generous in defeat, saying, 'You must give Aberdeen credit. They are a good team, they played well, and they took their chances. They thoroughly deserved their win.' He also vowed that his team would bounce back, starting with the Scottish Cup quarter-final the following weekend, even if Rangers still didn't know for sure who they were playing. The manager would attend the Rugby Park replay between Kilmarnock and Celtic on the Monday night, and he saw the Hoops' season slump from bad to worse when the First Division hosts enjoyed a shock 1-0 win. There would be no Old Firm hat-trick of fixtures; the visitors to Ibrox the following Saturday would be from Ayrshire, with an emotional return to his spiritual home for on-loan centre-forward Colin Stein, still an idol to the Ibrox faithful.

Much of the newspaper inches in the following days were devoted to the spectacular slump at Parkhead, with the previous season's champions staring at a battle to avoid relegation as they sat third from bottom of the table. The upcoming League Cup Final was their only chance of salvaging silverware from a campaign that saw the first doubts being expressed about Jock Stein's managerial ability. The crisis in the east end of the city overshadowed Kilmarnock's brilliant result, and also the build-up to the Scottish Cup quarter-finals. Over at Ibrox, Wallace confirmed in the midweek that Jardine was now over his injury and would be in the squad for the match. He did have a fresh injury worry, however, with Russell rated as highly doubtful.

By the Friday, Wallace revealed that Russell was out and that he would bring back the almost-forgotten Johnny Hamilton into the midfield. Hamilton, who had been a mainstay of the side in the previous two seasons, had asked for a transfer in January after slipping completely out of the first-team picture. His last competitive start had been in the Scottish Cup Final defeat at the end of 1976/77, and with another Old Firm final just a week later, he must have felt that the timing of his comeback couldn't have been better. 'Dingy', as he was known in the dressing room, seemed the most obvious direct replacement for Russell, whose intelligent and assured debut season had some pundits questioning why Scotland manager Ally McLeod had not included him in his provisional squad of 40 players for the World Cup finals in the summer. Wallace simply said, 'John has been playing well in the reserves. It's now up to him.'

Rangers v Kilmarnock
Saturday, 11 March 1978, Ibrox
Stewart Kennedy, Sandy Jardine, John Greig, Tom Forsyth, Colin Jackson, Alex MacDonald, Tommy McLean, Johnny Hamilton, Derek Johnstone, Gordon Smith, Davie Cooper
Substitutes: Derek Parlane, Alex Miller

A decent crowd of 28,000 included a noisy contingent from Ayrshire hoping to see their team complete the most unlikely Old Firm cup double in the space of just five days. It didn't take long for them to realise that Rangers were a very different proposition from their Glasgow rivals. Hamilton looked as if he had never been away, settling seamlessly into a midfield that quickly took control of the game. With Rangers dominating possession there was plenty service for the wingers, Davie Cooper in particular giving the Killie defence a torrid time. It also meant Colin Stein was given no opportunity to test his mates in the Rangers defence, the game passing him by after he had received a huge ovation before kick-off from the Ibrox crowd.

Cooper's tricks and crossing ability had the home crowd purring, but despite the good football and plenty of decent chances the first half ticked on with the visitors somehow holding out. The main man they had to thank for that was goalkeeper Jim Stewart, who showed why he was a contender for a seat on the plane to Argentina with Scotland in the summer. He defied Rangers with a string of good saves and confident catches, and with just five minutes remaining before half-time his manager Davie Sneddon must have started to think this just might be their day. Then the roof fell in.

Former Killie man Gordon Smith hit a speculative shot that should have been a routine save for Stewart, but after his earlier heroics the keeper made an awful mistake when he allowed the ball to cannon off his chest. On hand to punish him was fellow Scotland squad man Johnstone, who buried the rebound as Stewart held his head in his hands. Then, in the final minute of the half, Hamilton completed his return to favour by adding a terrific second goal, a rasping shot from all of 20 yards that gave Stewart no hope as it flew into the net just inside the left-hand post.

Two goals at the perfect time if you were a Rangers fan, but the Kilmarnock players trudged off at the interval knowing their cup dream had died. Their highly rated young winger Davie Provan never reappeared for the second half, his battle with the massively experienced John Greig something of a mismatch. It made no difference to the pattern of play, the second half being as one-sided as the first.

The only slight surprise was Kilmarnock reached the 67th minute without further loss, but when Rangers did eventually make it 3-0 they did so with a delightfully worked goal. Alex MacDonald took possession 40 yards out and played a clever pass to Hamilton, who was in some space. MacDonald then headed straight for the Kilmarnock penalty box for the return pass, with Hamilton on the same wavelength. He chipped it into space behind the central defence where MacDonald threw himself to connect with a perfect diving header that nestled in the corner of the net.

Rangers were now in cruise control and heading towards another Hampden semi-final. There was still time for two more goals before the crowd went home, however. In the 77th minute Cooper went past full-back Stuart McLean yet again, only for his progress to be halted when Stewart brought him crashing to the ground. It was as clear a penalty as you could wish to see, and Cooper rounded off his excellent display by confidently dispatching the spot-kick. Many of the visiting support took this as their cue to head for the exits, which meant the late consolation goal scored by midfielder Ian McCulloch received only very muted cheers.

After the disappointment of the Aberdeen defeat, it was a perfect response from Wallace's side, the manager beaming in the post-match interviews. He gave special praise to Cooper, who he described as the best winger in Scotland on his day. His performance wasn't enough to win the sponsors' man of the match award, however, with the £100 cheque going to Hamilton on his comeback. Wallace was equally delighted with the midfielder, who he confirmed would remain in the squad for the League Cup Final whether or not Bobby Russell recovered from illness.

Hamilton continued to make the headlines when he scored the only goal of a fiercely contested reserve fixture against Celtic on the Monday night in the Second XI Cup at Ibrox, a match that saw several recognised first-team players turn out for both sides. By then Rangers knew their opponents in the Scottish Cup semi-finals, with a Hampden date with Dundee United set for early April. Most observers were predicting a Rangers v Aberdeen final, with the top two teams in the country kept apart as Aberdeen had been drawn to play Partick Thistle.

That reserve cup tie had featured the skills of Bobby McKean on the right wing for Rangers, the former St Mirren player having recently been unable to force his way back into the first team after featuring often in the opening months of the season. Everyone at Ibrox was stunned on the morning of Thursday, 16 March when they were told of the devastating news that McKean had been found dead the previous day in the garage of his home in Barrhead. There was disbelief among his team-mates, the club management and the supporters at the news, the tragic loss of a highly talented and popular player at the age of just 25. Bobby had played an important role in two league championship wins in 1974/75 and 1975/76, as well as producing a memorable performance in the 1976 Scottish Cup Final win over Hearts where his imagination and trickery had created the clinching third goal for Derek Johnstone. He left behind a wife, a baby daughter, and countless memories in the shirt of the team he had always supported.

Probably in future years there would have been a request to postpone the cup final just two days later; the Rangers players had lost a close friend and colleague and this had to have a massive impact on them. But there was no alternative but to carry on the preparations for Hampden, and Russell started for the reserves that Thursday night against Clydebank to try to prove he was back to fitness in time for the big match. There was a minute's silence before the game, and Russell completed the 90 minutes, but he didn't look anywhere near his previous sharpness and Wallace had a big decision to make on who wore the number eight shirt against Celtic.

Just over 60,000 flocked to Hampden for the final on a crisp spring afternoon, the early 1pm kick-off now a regular feature of Old Firm matches. It was agreed that both teams would wear black armbands in memory of Bobby McKean, with the match preceded by a minute's silence.

Celtic v Rangers
Saturday, 18 March 1978, Hampden
Stewart Kennedy, Sandy Jardine, John Greig, Tom Forsyth, Colin Jackson, Alex MacDonald, Tommy McLean, Johnny Hamilton, Derek Johnstone, Gordon Smith, Davie Cooper
Substitutes: Derek Parlane, Alex Miller

Celtic were appearing in their 14th successive League Cup Final, a world record for any major domestic cup competition. Although this seemed a formidable record, they had only won six of the previous 13 showpieces, with just one victory in their last seven. Rangers were hot favourites, with two wins already over their old rivals during the season as well as a massive lead over them in the league table.

Wallace opted to go with the same team as the previous Saturday against Kilmarnock, with born-again Hamilton keeping his midfield berth. Although this was a huge disappointment for Russell, the elegant young midfielder knew deep down that he hadn't yet fully recovered from his recent illness and that he would have to wait before making his first cup final appearance for the club.

After the usual pre-match presentations, the silence to mark the tragic passing of Bobby McKean was started. Sadly it was marred by several unsavoury chants from the terraces occupied by the Celtic support, this inhuman response to a human tragedy doing nothing to dampen the hostility between the two sets of supporters. The silence was brought to a premature end with the Rangers fans making their anger and disgust loudly known. It was a shameful start to a showpiece occasion.

The match itself started cagily, as is often the case in major finals. Referee David Syme was as busy as any of the players in the opening exchanges, in what was the first final of his officiating career. It took almost 20 minutes for the first meaningful attempt at goal and it came at the Rangers end. Young Celtic midfielder Roy Aitken drove forward and saw his goalbound shot brilliantly turned round the post by Stewart Kennedy. This scare prompted the first sustained period of Rangers pressure, and five minutes later it looked as if the favourites had taken the lead.

John Greig powered down the left and played the ball into the Celtic penalty box. It eventually fell at the feet of Johnstone some 12 yards out, and he expertly dispatched it past Peter Latchford to prompt mass celebrations behind the goal. Then, to the astonishment of most inside the stadium, Syme ruled out the goal, awarding instead a free kick to Celtic on the byline. The 'offence' that he had spotted was Greig stepping off the field of play so he would not be judged offside while the play developed in the goalmouth. This was deemed ungentlemanly conduct, and an indirect free kick to Celtic was awarded. Fair to say that virtually no player or spectator had seen this decision made before, nor would they ever see it again.

It was a massive escape for Celtic and they almost took advantage of it in the 37th minute when Kennedy seemed hesitant trying to stop a Ronnie Glavin shot, the ball rebounding off his chest before being smuggled to safety. Within 60 seconds of this the ball was in the Celtic net again, and this time it counted. Gordon Smith took on Glavin on the Rangers left, but appeared at first to overrun the ball. Glavin tried to shepherd the ball out over the goal line but Smith managed to hook it across goal. His cross was met ten yards out by the left foot of Cooper who swept an unstoppable shot high past Latchford, Johnstone doing well to leap out of the way of the ball as it thundered towards goal.

Two of the summer signings who had transformed the Rangers team had combined to put them in front, and they kept their lead until half-time despite some Celtic pressure as they responded to going a goal down.

Celtic started the second period on the offensive, their whole season now on the line as the only trophy they could still win was slipping away from them. Kennedy produced another fine save, this time from a George McCluskey header, but it started to look more and more as if that one goal would be enough. In a sign of their increasing desperation, Celtic skipper Andy Lynch was booked for starting a needless pushing match with the diminutive Tommy McLean, the Rangers man's name also going into the book as he shoved back in retaliation.

The songs of victory were starting to be sung from the Rangers end when out of nowhere Celtic levelled the scores with just six minutes to go. Full-back Alan Sneddon sent in a high looping cross from the right which should have been a routine catch for Kennedy. Inexplicably, the big goalkeeper totally misjudged the flight, allowing it to sail over his arms, and in behind him ran Jóhannes Eðvaldsson who nodded the ball into the empty Rangers net off the crossbar.

There had been a few in the Celtic end who had started drifting to the exits but they were stopped in their tracks by this unexpected turn of events, and it was the turn of those in green to celebrate wildly and find their singing voices. Rangers had one last chance to snatch the cup but Latchford saved well from a McLean free kick. It meant extra time, with Wallace and Stein on the pitch at full time to demand even more effort from their tiring players.

The extra time period was more notable for nervy football and fouls than it was for goalmouth incident. Both sides seemed scared to throw too many men forward and a stalemate developed. Wallace threw on both substitutes, goalscorer Cooper making way for Derek Parlane and Alex Miller replacing Hamilton. The arrival of Parlane was to give Rangers added goal threat, but it was the other substitute who was involved in the deciding moment of the game.

There had been 117 minutes played when Miller crossed into the Celtic area from the right. Latchford rose to collect it, with MacDonald bursting into the penalty box and leaping alongside the goalkeeper. The midfielder's presence unnerved Latchford, who punched the ball weakly. It dropped in front of Smith, 14 yards out, and he became the hero of the day by diving to head back into the empty net. The Celtic players sank to their knees; there was no way back with so little time left and they watched on as the men in blue mobbed the goalscorer.

Stein raced from his dugout, suggesting to the officials that MacDonald had impeded his goalkeeper, but television

The three new arrivals at Ibrox who helped transform Rangers in 1977/78 – Gordon Smith, Davie Cooper and Bobby Russell. (Courtesy of Rangers FC)

Bobby McKean in the 3-2 comeback win over Celtic in September 1977.

Arnold Muhren scores the second goal in FC Twente's 3-0 victory that sent Rangers out of Europe at the end of September.

Furious Celtic players surround the referee after John Greig's controversial goal in the 3-1 January win in the Old Firm match at Ibrox.

Davie Cooper opens the scoring in the League Cup Final against Celtic.

Gordon Smith dives to head home the dramatic late winner in the League Cup Final. (Courtesy of Rangers FC)

League Cup-winning manager Jock Wallace and captain John Greig are interviewed post-match by Archie Macpherson for the BBC.

Iconic Old Firm managers Jock Wallace and Jock Stein prior to their last-ever Old Firm clash at Parkhead in March 1978.

Rod Stewart promotes the upcoming John Greig testimonial match by wearing the famous red, white and blue.

The 'Greatest Ranger' waves to 65,000 fans before the start of his testimonial match in April 1978.

Sandy Jardine in a race with his Scotland colleague John Robertson during the John Greig testimonial match.

John Greig is carried shoulder high after leading his team to the title by beating Motherwell at Ibrox. (Courtesy of Rangers FC)

The Cup Final squad pose for a team picture as they prepare for Hampden and a possible treble. (Courtesy of Rangers FC)

Alex MacDonald has opened the scoring in the Scottish Cup Final, and Davie Cooper joins in the celebrations.

Derek Johnstone's bullet header has put Rangers 2-0 up in the Scottish Cup Final.

The Rangers bench celebrate as the final whistle sounds in the Scottish Cup Final and the treble is confirmed.

Dejection for Aberdeen manager Billy McNeill and captain Willie Miller as they watch the Rangers players celebrate.

The victorious treble winners enjoy their lap of honour after winning the Scottish Cup.

Captain Greig and top scorer Johnstone pose with the Scottish Cup. Neither would know they would soon be Rangers manager and captain.

The Ibrox stadium of 1977/78 that would now undergo a transformation into one of the most modern arenas in UK football.

pictures later would confirm there was no contact between the players. The Celtic boss wouldn't let this lie, and on the final whistle he angrily confronted Syme, with whatever he said later resulting in a £200 fine from the SFA. In contrast, Wallace was happily embracing every one of his players, with Smith almost smothered by his ecstatic manager.

In truth, Rangers hadn't played well, but they had done what all great teams did when it mattered. They had found a way to win. Most observers felt that Celtic had done enough to earn a replay, but all the men from Parkhead now had to look forward to was pulling away from the relegation zone and watching on as Rangers tried to claim all of Scotland's major prizes.

After the match, Sandy Jardine presented his medal to Bobby Russell, telling the youngster that he deserved it for how he had played in his debut season. It was a sign of the great team spirit in the dressing room. Russell said, 'It helped me get over the disappointment of not playing, although seeing Rangers win the cup was the most important thing of all.' Wallace added, 'All the lads appreciated how young Robert felt. Sandy was first to say he would give him his medal, and I thought a lot of him for doing that. It's the way we try to be at Ibrox.'

There was little time for the cup-winning celebrations, with a rearranged league fixture against Partick Thistle at Ibrox to be played on the Tuesday night. Wallace told reporters that Russell would be added to the 13 players who had played at Hampden, but a late decision would be made on his fitness. As well as winning the League Cup, it had been a good weekend for Rangers in the title race with Aberdeen drawing 0-0 with Dundee United. This meant their lead at the top was down to three points, but crucially Rangers had played a game fewer. With Aberdeen also in action against lowly Clydebank, a win was vital before the visit to Parkhead on the Saturday.

Rangers v Partick Thistle
Tuesday, 21 March 1978, Ibrox
Stewart Kennedy, Sandy Jardine, John Greig, Tom Forsyth, Colin Jackson, Alex MacDonald, Tommy McLean, Johnny Hamilton, Derek Johnstone, Gordon Smith, Davie Cooper
Substitutes: Derek Parlane, Alex Miller

Bobby Russell wasn't risked, a sensible decision with some huge games on the horizon. It was the cup-winning team who took to the field in front of a disappointing crowd of around 15,000. Apart from the match itself, a big talking point of the day was the SFA meeting that had been held to discuss the issue of pitch invasions by fans. Motherwell had asked in a letter for Rangers to be deducted two points for the events at Fir Park during the 5-3 win in February; the association declined to take such drastic action but did agree to an enquiry into the match, with match officials and club representatives asked to attend.

Before kick-off the team paraded the League Cup to the fans, although with the crowd so sparse it didn't seem to be the most celebratory occasion. The match programme featured a club statement on the death of Bobby McKean, his loss still felt deeply inside Ibrox.

The game itself quickly became a battle between the Rangers attack and a packed Thistle defence. Firhill boss Bertie Auld had decided on an ultra-defensive formation after some poor recent results, with Ian Gibson and John Marr deployed as man-to-man markers on Alex MacDonald and Gordon Smith. This stifling approach presented Rangers with a real problem and the two players who timed

MARCH: TRAGEDY AND TRIUMPH

their penalty box runs to support Derek Johnstone both struggled to find any room to influence proceedings in the early stages. It was an approach that was seen more often in two-legged European competition than domestic league football, and at half-time Auld would have justification in saying he had been vindicated.

The teams returned to the dressing rooms with no goals on the scoreboard, although this had as much to do with a couple of terrible misses as it had to do with expert defending. Unusually, it was the two Ibrox top goalscorers who were the guilty men. Midway through the half, Scotland's number one goalkeeper Alan Rough totally misjudged a cross, leaving Johnstone unmarked and with an open goal to head into. To the amazement of everyone inside Ibrox, the man who was regarded as the best aerial menace in the country headed wide. Then ten minutes later, Smith escaped the clutches of Marr for the first time and got on the end of a precise McLean pass with just Rough to beat from ten yards. The cup final hero also failed to hit the target, blazing his effort well over.

The second half started out as a copy of the first – all Rangers possession, Thistle forward Doug Somner left all alone up front, and the fans growing more restless. But finally the deadlock was broken after 51 minutes as Auld's plan started to crumble. Recent Thistle signing Colin McAdam, who had been having a terrific battle with Johnstone, failed to properly clear a McLean cross, miscuing it back across the face of his own goal. First to the loose ball was MacDonald, that ever-dependable scorer of important goals, and he evaded his marker by diving full length to head the ball past Rough.

The cheers of relief from the home fans sparked a rethink in the away dugout, Thistle now ordered to abandon their previous defensive shell and get forward. They failed to trouble the experienced Rangers defence, however, and with 15 minutes left it looked for all the world like a 1-0 home win. Then, out of nowhere, a George Mackie hopeful cross into the Rangers area saw Somner outjump Colin Jackson and bullet home a header. Auld celebrated as if his team had just won the cup final, and Rangers were looking at a damaging dent in their title hopes.

Both Derek Parlane and Alex Miller came off the bench to replace Hamilton and McLean as Rangers started running out of time. It would have been a travesty if Thistle's 'anti-football' had won them a point, and injustice was avoided in the very last minute of normal time. Yet another cross into the Partick box was cleared, but this time it fell at the feet of Sandy Jardine, who was up supporting his attack. The Scotland right-back controlled the ball instantly, took a stride forward, then drilled a low, hard shot past Rough and into the corner of the net. The small crowd erupted, the roar of joy much louder than seemed possible with their numbers. McAdam chased referee Ken Stewart back to the halfway line, protesting at an infringement when the initial cross had been cleared, but it wasn't clear what offence he was claiming to exist.

The final whistle sounded moments later, with the Rangers players raising their arms aloft, showing how important they felt this win would be. Aberdeen also won, so the lead remained the same before the trip to Parkhead. Celtic, meantime, lost yet again, this time going down at Fir Park, meaning they would kick-off the Old Firm match in the unbelievable position of third from bottom.

With the cup final win and the very different league campaigns, Jock Wallace was asked about his team being strong favourites for the match and whether he had to guard against overconfidence. He replied simply, 'The League Cup is done. We now have to concentrate on staying ahead of Aberdeen in the league, and we do that by beating Celtic. We have no other thoughts.'

Celtic v Rangers
Saturday, 25 March 1978, Celtic Park
Stewart Kennedy, Sandy Jardine, John Greig, Tom Forsyth, Colin Jackson, Alex MacDonald, Tommy McLean, Bobby Russell, Derek Johnstone, Gordon Smith, Davie Cooper
Substitutes: Derek Parlane, Alex Miller

It was a sign of the despondency of the Celtic support that stand tickets were still on sale on the morning of the match, and the confidence of the Rangers fans increased even further when they saw that Bobby Russell was back in the number eight shirt, replacing Johnny Hamilton. At 21 years of age, Russell had been so impressive in his first season that he was regarded as an automatic choice by most of the Ibrox faithful. It represented something of a gamble, however, with the player not having built back his match sharpness after his illness.

In the end, a decent crowd of 50,000 was given as the attendance, and it was a game that those packed into the visiting end would want to quickly forget. Right from kick-off Rangers looked lethargic and off the pace, with Celtic in contrast playing as if their lives depended on a result. The home support quickly got behind their fallen heroes as they exerted serious pressure on the Rangers goal. Within the first quarter of an hour they had created three decent opportunities. First, Roy Aitken miskicked when in a great position, then Johnny Doyle fired in a fierce 20-yarder that Stewart Kennedy did well to stop. Aitken was the sinner the next time, firing wildly over the crossbar when he had time to do better.

It was quickly becoming obvious that Russell wasn't ready for a match of this ferocity and he looked a shadow of the midfield general that had dominated so many games before his illness. With the midfield being overrun, it was left to the defence to try to hold back the attacking tide towards them and both Tom Forsyth and Colin Jackson showed their experience by making crucial interventions. As the half hour passed some in the Rangers end may have thought they had survived the onslaught, but in the 32nd minute Celtic took a deserved lead. The goal was a personal nightmare for Kennedy. The former Scotland man should have easily stopped a long-range Ronnie Glavin shot that had direction but seemed to lack the power to score from so far out. Inexplicably Kennedy, after looking to have the shot covered, allowed the ball to squirm under his hands and into the net.

Glavin jumped for joy, probably as much in surprise as in delight. Rangers were finally stung into some kind of action and they finally tested Celtic goalkeeper Peter Latchford a few minutes later when he did well to save a firmly struck Davie Cooper free kick. In truth it was about the first time Cooper had been seen as an attacking threat all day, and two minutes later the threat was again at the other end. A Celtic free kick was played into the Rangers penalty box where it was controlled by Jóhannes Eðvaldsson. Surrounded by defenders, he flicked the ball to his defensive partner Roddie MacDonald and the big centre-back smashed the ball past Kennedy to make it 2-0.

Neither set of fans could believe what they were watching, with those in blue now stunned into near silence. The Celtic fans gave their men a huge ovation as the teams left the pitch moments later, Jock Wallace looking fit to explode as he stormed up the tunnel. It was a surprise to see the same 11 start the second half, Wallace seemingly content to allow the 11 players who put Rangers into this hole to dig them back out.

But although the match was far more even in the second period, Celtic seemed content to defend and rarely did they look in danger of surrendering their advantage. Derek Parlane and Alex Miller were finally given the nod to join the fray after 64 minutes, it being no surprise to see Cooper and Russell replaced. Captain John Greig let his frustration get the better of him and was booked by referee Ian Foote for a crunching tackle on Doyle as Rangers slipped to a now inevitable defeat. They did at least test Latchford a few times in the closing stages, the English goalkeeper making one excellent save from substitute Parlane.

It ended 2-0 with Rangers having no room for complaint on the day. Things got even worse when news filtered through from up north that Aberdeen had beaten Ayr United 4-1, which meant that the lead was now down to a single point. The game in hand that Rangers had was now looking ever more important, albeit it was a tricky trip to Tannadice which had no firm date to be played as yet. There was another tricky away game next, however, with an in-form Hibs at Easter Road the next opponents in midweek. After starting the month as seeming title certainties, the Rangers supporters were now more than a little nervous.

As the new week arrived, Wallace told reporters there was no point in mulling over the weekend horror show. 'When you've taken a knock the only thing to do is come fighting back,' he growled. But there was no doubt that the manager was seething behind the scenes, and many observers were predicting changes in the line-up in Edinburgh.

The unexpected slip-up at Parkhead had restored interest in the betting market. Rangers, who had been as little as 1/7 favourites, were now a more attractive 1/2, still strong favourites but no longer racing certainties. Meanwhile, Billy McNeill's Aberdeen had seen their odds shorten down to just 7/4, and they were now also being quoted at 7/1 for a league and cup double. Wallace's dilemma over team selection was confirmed when he took the unusual step of naming a 16-man squad to take to Easter Road, adding Johnny Hamilton, Kenny Watson and Peter McCloy to the travelling party. The addition of a second goalkeeper fuelled speculation that Kennedy could be about to pay for his clanger at the weekend with his place in the team.

On the afternoon of the match, news emerged from SFA headquarters that the Disciplinary and Referee Committee had recommended that the controversial Motherwell v Rangers match at Fir Park in late February be replayed due to the pitch invasion by Rangers supporters. A stunned Willie Waddell would only say, 'We are awaiting a full report of this recommendation, and when we have that report it will be discussed at board level.' He refused to give any personal opinion on this bombshell news, although it seemed pretty obvious that this was a decision Rangers would strongly challenge. Meanwhile, there was a match to be played, and a vital two points to be won.

Hibs v Rangers
Wednesday, 29 March 1978, Easter Road
Peter McCloy, Sandy Jardine, John Greig, Tom Forsyth, Colin Jackson, Alex MacDonald, Tommy McLean, Johnny Hamilton, Derek Johnstone, Gordon Smith, Derek Parlane
Substitutes: Davie Cooper, Alex Miller

MARCH: TRAGEDY AND TRIUMPH

The manager's unhappiness after the abject display at Parkhead was made obvious when the team was finally revealed. Three changes were made, none of them due to injury. Stewart Kennedy paid for his howler for the first Celtic goal by losing his place, with Davie Cooper benched after Derek Parlane had shown far more threat in his brief appearance in the derby defeat. Wallace also dropped Bobby Russell and restored Johnny Hamilton, perhaps admitting he had rushed the youngster back too quickly. With every point now a prisoner, he had to hope this rejigged team would gel straight away.

Parlane and Johnstone were the twin strikeforce, with Gordon Smith moving out wide to become more the Cooper replacement. With Hibs in fine form, a noisy crowd of over 21,000 assembled at Easter Road hoping to see a cracking advert for Scottish football. Instead most went home talking about the man in the middle.

Referee Bob Valentine was a busy man from the start as firm tackles flew in from both sides, both looking to assert themselves on the opposition. Valentine seemed unwilling to clamp down as things got progressively more physical, and by the time he belatedly decided action was required he had lost control. It didn't help the official that Hibs seemed determined to claim for a penalty for any contact in the Rangers box, with players and fans showing their displeasure when their shouts for a spot-kick were denied. In fairness, among several claims there did look to be one where they were justified in being unhappy, Rangers somewhat fortunate not to see Valentine point to the spot.

In among the battles, Rangers were the ones who created the best chances. Parlane really should have scored when set free of the Hibs defence by partner Johnstone, but the striker lost his composure and fired his shot too high. Gradually the home team started to press forward themselves, but after 35 minutes Arthur Duncan was punished for a moment of slackness. He dallied in possession and was robbed, then the ball was quickly played forward and into the Hibs area. Johnstone rose highest and cushioned a header down into the path of his strike partner, and Parlane didn't miss this time by sending a fierce first-time drive past goalkeeper Mike McDonald.

The goalscorer was booked a minute later for a late tackle on his marker George Stewart, and this would later prove to be a pivotal moment in the match. At half-time, however, it was the away support who enjoyed their Bovril more, their team holding a vital lead in a vital match. The home fans were more concerned with letting Valentine know what they thought of him, with some of the wiser heads in the travelling support worried that the referee might try to even things up after the break.

After an early second-half booking for Hibs striker Ally McLeod for a lunge at Alex MacDonald, the match descended into mayhem just after the hour. Hibs defender Jackie McNamara tangled with Parlane and seemed to throw the Rangers man to the ground. Players from both sides rushed to the scene and it took the match officials some time to restore some semblance of order. Once the pushing and shoving had stopped, Valentine showed the yellow card to McNamara and sent Parlane off. The Rangers man, along with his team-mates and his manager, looked totally stunned. With fans on both sides now in a frenzy, and with tempers now boiling over, it was going to be a red-hot last 28 minutes.

Wallace tried to reorganise his ten men, withdrawing winger Tommy McLean for the more defensive Alex Miller, with the intent now obvious that they were looking to protect their lead against the 11 men in green and white. With Tom Forsyth in particular standing tall against the Hibs attacks, and with McCloy coping well with anything coming his way, Rangers held out until 11 minutes from the end. They were undone by another baffling decision by the hapless Valentine. Striker Tony Higgins fell theatrically under a Forsyth challenge, with even the Hibs fans not impressed. Incredibly, the referee gave a penalty. Not only did Forsyth and his colleagues complain bitterly that there had been no contact on Higgins, they also legitimately pointed out that the coming together was well outside the penalty box anyway.

The Rangers fans were in a rage at the man in black, who had robbed them of the Scottish Cup Final against Celtic at the end of the previous season with another contentious penalty award. After the protests were waved away, McLeod kept his head to tuck the penalty past McCloy and to ensure a share of the points, the big goalkeeper getting fingertips to the ball but unable to keep it out.

The 1-1 draw, coupled with Aberdeen's 2-1 win at Love Street, meant the Dons were now the league leaders, topping the table on goal difference with both teams on 43 points. Rangers had seven games left to play, with the new leaders one fewer. This was on the proviso that the two points gained at Fir Park in February still stood.

Wallace was almost lost for words after the match, but it was telling that he was quick to point out that Parlane would not be disciplined by the club for his dismissal, despite a club policy of fining players for red cards. That told the world what he thought of the match-changing decision.

The following day, Willie Waddell confirmed that the club would 'fight all the way' the decision to replay the Motherwell clash, his anger evident when explaining the club's stance to the press. The general manager pointed out that the referee and both clubs were satisfied on the day of the result, as were the Scottish League, and that Rangers felt 'victimised' by the SFA for this unprecedented decision. He also spoke of the post-match interview given by Motherwell boss Roger Hynd where he had said that the pitch invasion had not affected the result, and that the better team had won the game. It seemed obvious there was a collision to come between the country's biggest club and the national association when Waddell added, 'The referee's initial report on the match could not have possibly guided the committee to make this decision. There have been many pitch invasions in Scottish football in recent times and little has been said about them. Why should we be sitting ducks? It is little short of victimisation.' Waddell ended his angry press conference by declaring on behalf of the players, the management, and the vast majority of decent Rangers supporters, 'Under no circumstances will we back down on this issue.'

March started with Rangers serenely on course for treble glory. They won a trophy but lost a popular player in tragic circumstances. And the month ended with the club in the middle of a titanic battle on and off the pitch. March would be remembered for many reasons, and it looked like April would be a defining month.

10

April: A Captain's Tale

THE FIRST match of the title run-in was at home to St Mirren. The Rangers fans would likely also have an eye on events across the city, with Aberdeen visiting Parkhead in what looked to be their toughest remaining fixture. But Jock Wallace only had his mind on the visit of Alex Ferguson's talented young team; with Rangers dropping five points in their last four matches it was time to steady the ship.

Wallace decided Bobby Russell would get 90 minutes in the reserves at Paisley with a view to proving his match sharpness for the midweek Scottish Cup semi-final. His plan was dashed, however, when the Love Street pitch was declared unplayable, meaning his influential midfielder sat out the action completely.

Rangers v St Mirren
Saturday, 1 April 1978, Ibrox
Peter McCloy, Sandy Jardine, John Greig, Tom Forsyth, Colin Jackson, Alex MacDonald, Tommy McLean, Johnny Hamilton, Derek Johnstone, Gordon Smith, Derek Parlane
Substitutes: Davie Cooper, Alex Miller

It was 'same again' for Rangers, despite many on the terraces worried about a lack of creativity without Russell and Davie Cooper, and with Gordon Smith playing out wide. That concern seemed to be eased in the early stages with the two Dereks up front both having good chances to score. But the visitors looked well balanced in midfield and gradually started to win the battle in the engine room, Rangers still feeling the absence of Russell. Saints were getting forward themselves, and in the 20th minute they had a glorious chance to take the lead and pile more misery on the 20,000 home crowd.

Colin Jackson was short with a back-pass, allowing centre-forward Frank McGarvey to get to the ball ahead of Peter McCloy. The big goalkeeper got there second and knocked McGarvey to the ground when trying to win the ball. Unlike at Easter Road, this one was an obvious penalty, referee George Smith correctly awarding it. When former Rangers player Iain Munro stepped up to take the kick, captain John Greig ran to his goalkeeper with words of advice. Perhaps he remembered from training alongside Munro his favoured penalty technique, as his advice did the trick. McCloy cemented his return to the number one jersey by saving the effort to huge cheers from the Ibrox crowd.

But despite this escape, Rangers still struggled to find any fluency with the visitors increasingly taking control. Their young and industrious midfield impressed all who were watching, with Tony Fitzpatrick particularly impressive. Wallace would have been hoping to get his team into the dressing room at 0-0, but with less than two minutes before referee Smith could call a halt, Saints grabbed a deserved lead. The scorer was McGarvey, another young player who was being tipped for greater things. He showed excellent control to sidestep a Jackson tackle before firing a low shot beyond the despairing dive of McCloy.

The Rangers support were now in despair, watching on as the season looked to be unravelling before them. But Wallace always spoke of the character of his players, and they showed they weren't willing to lie down when they roared upfield and equalised right on the stroke of half-time. It was a very familiar goal, a Tommy McLean cross headed past Alan McCulloch by top scorer Johnstone.

At half-time the supporters listened to general manager Willie Waddell, who strode out on the turf to address the fans on the club's position on the Motherwell replay decision by the SFA. He repeated his strong words from the midweek press conference, insisting that the club's players should not and would not be punished for actions that were nothing to do with them. The fans gave their vocal backing to his every word.

News also emerged from Parkhead that Celtic were leading Aberdeen 1-0, and all of a sudden there was optimism inside Ibrox that the team were on their way back to the top of the table. A win could now be crucial, but if the fans expected Rangers to now grab the game by the throat they were to be disappointed. St Mirren continued to hold the upper hand, albeit McCloy didn't have to produce any heroics to prevent them taking the lead.

With the game petering out towards a draw, both teams then had the chance to grab the points in the closing stages. First, Jackson managed to clear a goalbound effort off the line with his goalkeeper beaten, with the referee then being chased by a few Saints players who were adamant the ball had crossed the line before the centre-half hooked it away. Then, with just two minutes left, Smith somehow screwed a shot wide from just four yards out with the goal gaping.

A 1-1 draw saw yet another point dropped, Rangers now having won just once in their last five league outings. Aberdeen fought back to grab a point against Celtic so it was 'as you were' at the top, but with the Dons having played what looked like the much tougher fixture. The bookmakers still had Rangers as odds-on favourites for the title but there was no doubt that Aberdeen were in better form, and there were plenty of worried faces leaving Ibrox to head home. Rangers had six league matches left to play, with the game in hand looking crucial, regardless of whether a replayed trip to Motherwell would need to happen.

League business then had to go on the backburner as there was now the small matter of a Scottish Cup semi-final to play in midweek at Hampden against Dundee United. With just two goals scored in the last three games, Wallace put his team through extra shooting practice on the Monday, watched by a delegation of Italian coaches who were the guests of the SFA director of coaching Andy Roxburgh. They saw Bobby Russell take full part in the session, with Wallace desperate to have his midfield lynchpin back in the team for the Hampden showdown.

Wallace and his Tannadice counterpart Jim McLean spoke to the press the day before the semi-final, both men confident that their team would progress to the final at the start of May. At Ibrox the players were described as 'looking good', as Wallace growled about their lack of killer instinct in front of goal and how this was his focus in training. On Tayside, McLean spoke of his young players being a match for their more illustrious opponents, with his only concern being their mental toughness on the big occasion. He stated, 'Rangers have more problems than we have. We have youngsters hungry for success and we can play as well as anyone. But we must match Rangers in their will to win, as only then can our skill count for anything.'

The pressure on Rangers increased further the night before the match, Aberdeen defeating Partick Thistle in a league game and moving two points clear at the top of the table. A crowd of 25,000 made the journey to Hampden, the vast majority wearing blue and hoping that their team could find their form again.

Rangers v Dundee United
Wednesday, 5 April 1978, Hampden
Peter McCloy, Sandy Jardine, John Greig, Tom Forsyth, Colin Jackson, Alex MacDonald, Tommy McLean, Bobby Russell, Derek Johnstone, Gordon Smith, Davie Cooper
Substitutes: Derek Parlane, Alex Miller

With the return of both Russell and Cooper to the starting 11, the team was now back to what many saw as the best available. United were also at full strength as a reported injury scare to talented sweeper David Narey had proved to be inaccurate and he took his usual place in the back four. History certainly favoured Rangers, who were looking to bring the cup back to Ibrox for the 22nd time while their opponents had never lifted the trophy. United, in fact, were looking for their first victory over Rangers in the competition.

That tradition seemed to matter for little in the first half as United dominated for long spells. Rangers looked nervous, their recent poor run noticeably affecting their confidence, with the defence in particular jittery when put under pressure. Striker John Bourke thought he had given the Tannadice men a dream start but his effort was cleared off the line by Jackson with McCloy beaten. This was a second crucial goal-line intervention by the big centre-half in the space of four days, although the response from the terraces was more of frustration than gratitude.

By the time the interval arrived Rangers had hardly mustered a worthwhile goal attempt, whereas both Paul Sturrock and John Holt had missed glaring chances to add to the misery of the Ibrox punters. There were several boos as the teams left the field, Rangers looking like a team who badly needed a spark of imagination to inspire them back into their groove. The one bright spot had been the return of Russell, who showed glimpses of his old form when able to get on the ball.

Some in the crowd may have expected a substitution at half-time, but the same 11 players lined up for the second half – and the next 25 minutes were more of the same with United enjoying most possession and looking clever on the ball, while Rangers were disjointed and failing to mount any serious assault on Hamish McAlpine's goal. In the 70th minute Derek Johnstone picked out Russell making a run down the wing. As Johnstone then hared into the penalty box hoping for the cross to come his way, a chorus of 'What a load of rubbish' started among some of the disgruntled Rangers fans. Russell ignored this and sent in a beautiful teasing cross to the back post, where Johnstone was on hand to flash a powerful header past McAlpine and into the net.

The mood changed instantly, Johnstone taking the acclaim of the same supporters who had jeered seconds before. The small band of United fans were in disbelief that their team were behind after looking to be in total control; perhaps their manager's fears about his players' mentality were justified. In contrast, there seemed to be a visible weight lifted from the shoulders of the Rangers players, and they went for the kill.

Wallace immediately sent on Alex Miller for Davie Cooper, and just eight minutes later Rangers' place in the final was secure after a goal fit to win any cup tie. Referee Ian Foote awarded a free kick, which was chipped towards the United penalty box by Tommy McLean. It was perfectly judged to match the run of John Greig, who had sprinted forward from his defensive position. The captain controlled the ball on his chest, brushed aside a challenging defender, then hooked a tremendous shot past McAlpine to a thunderous roar from the Rangers end. The 35-year-old Ibrox legend could add another moment of inspiration to the countless others he had given to the cause over his incredible career. And what a way to start his testimonial month.

This allowed Wallace to take off the limping Johnstone and give Derek Parlane the final few minutes. With the title run-in now well under way, all those in blue hoped that the team's top scorer hadn't picked up a significant injury. Rangers had given the young pretenders a harsh lesson, scoring with their first real chances of the game. They comfortably played out the closing stages with the song now favoured by the fans being 'We're going to win the cup'. A lot can change in 20 minutes when following Rangers!

Russell was awarded the sponsors' man of the match prize, and his manager sang his praises after the match. Wallace also singled out Cooper, who he claimed had produced 'his best game since joining Rangers'. With the cup final on Saturday, 6 May to look forward to, Wallace could now fully focus his players on winning the Premier Division, which he made clear was the number one priority. 'These players have come through a sticky spell,' he said. 'But they have not had one word of criticism from me. The target now is the championship. It doesn't bother me that Aberdeen are being talked up. What we do is entirely up to us.'

Rangers had a trip to Ayr next on the horizon, with the hosts deep in relegation trouble. This looked an ideal game to get the title challenge back on track, with Aberdeen again playing Partick Thistle, this time at Firhill. In an unusual fixture scheduling twist, the teams were then to play each other again the following midweek, with Ayr visiting Ibrox in one of Rangers' games in hand, while the Dons and the Jags were to contest the other Scottish Cup semi-final.

Wallace delayed naming his side for the trip to Ayrshire, giving Johnstone right up until the morning of the match to shake off the thigh injury he picked up at Hampden. He insisted that Ayr presented a tough challenge despite their league position, warning that Rangers had endured some tough results at Somerset Park over recent years.

Ayr United v Rangers
Saturday, 8 April 1978, Somerset Park
Peter McCloy, Sandy Jardine, John Greig, Tom Forsyth, Colin Jackson, Alex MacDonald, Tommy McLean, Bobby Russell, Derek Johnstone, Gordon Smith, Davie Cooper
Substitutes: Derek Parlane, Alex Miller

With Derek Johnstone passed fit, it was an unchanged Rangers who took to the muddy Somerset Park pitch in front of over 13,000 fans. In goal for Ayr United was Hugh Sproat, a larger-than-life character who enjoyed plenty banter with the away fans. As was his custom, he wore an emerald green top to face Rangers, although he donned a more fetching blue jersey whenever Celtic were in town!

If the big away following were thinking that their team were now back to their confident best after the midweek victory, they soon were forced into a rethink. Rangers started the game badly, allowing the home team to carve out several chances. And in just four minutes they took one of them, goalscorer Davie McCulloch giving McCloy no chance. The home fans were in dreamland, and wasted no time in taunting their visitors with chants suggesting Aberdeen were going to win the title. Rangers were doing little to prove them wrong in the opening half an hour, struggling to build any rhythm in their play on a difficult surface. It took a moment of controversy for the match to turn.

Cooper played in an in-swinging corner, with Johnstone rising highest to head the ball into goal. Defender Robert Connor attempted a last-gasp goal-line clearance but referee John Gordon immediately signalled the ball had crossed the line and Rangers had equalised. This decision was the cue for mass protests from the Ayr players, with Sproat seemingly telling the official that he had been impeded going for the cross, while Connor was adamant he had managed to hook the ball to safety just in time. Neither argument cut any ice with the official and the scores were level.

None in the ground could be certain whether the referee called it right, but it was fair to say that Gordon had a better view than most. No matter the circumstances, the goal had come at just the right time as players and fans alike had started to show their frustration. Six minutes later that was forgotten completely, as Greig again showed what a leader he was. The skipper, his testimonial match now just eight days away, took possession 40 yards out and ran at the Ayr defence. He played a one-two with Johnstone, burst into the penalty box, then took advantage of a deflection off a defender to hammer an unstoppable shot high past Sproat. In the space of three days Greig had shown why he would go down in history as one of the club's all-time greatest players.

His will to win and absolute dedication to the cause had been the difference in so many battles over so many years, and if anyone was going to drag Rangers over the winning line it would be John Greig MBE.

The Ayr players left the pitch at half-time still complaining to the referee, and probably realising that their chance of an upset had gone. Their fears were justified as the second half turned into something of a procession with Rangers free of the nerves that had affected them in the early stages and knocking the ball around in some style.

Gordon Smith found space in the home penalty area to bury the ball past Sproat just eight minutes after the resumption, and it now looked like a case of how many. Johnstone was causing havoc in the Ayr penalty area, dominating in the air against centre-half Rikki Fleming, and it came as no surprise in the 68th minute when the deadly striker struck his second goal of the game. It was also no surprise that it was a thumping header.

With over 20 minutes left Rangers had the chance to do their goal difference some good, which might prove invaluable in such a tight race. There were still 12 minutes to play when Smith completed his double, with cries of 'We're going to win the league' ringing around Somerset Park as the beleaguered home players again restarted the match. Rangers looked in the mood for even more, but sloppiness at the back in the closing minutes saw Gordon slightly appease the home fans by awarding a penalty. Brian McLaughlin made no mistake from the spot, leaving the final score as 5-2, and ensuring Rangers were still two points behind Aberdeen as the league leaders had won 2-0 at Firhill.

This meant another three-goal win over the same opponents at Ibrox on the Wednesday night would be enough for Rangers to reclaim top spot, the fans confident

APRIL: A CAPTAIN'S TALE

that this would happen after such a one-sided second half.

Sandy Jardine and Derek Johnstone didn't have the rest of the weekend off and instead travelled down to London along with several other members of the Scotland squad to record backing vocals for the official World Cup song, a Rod Stewart effort entitled 'Ole, Ola'. Stewart didn't join the players at the recording studio; he was represented by a life-sized cardboard cut-out with his vocals already recorded in Los Angeles. With Andy Cameron's 'Ally's Tartan Army' already having sold 300,000 copies, there was no doubt that World Cup fever was sweeping the country.

On the Monday, the SFA Referees Committee met to discuss Rangers' appeal against their decision to replay the match against Motherwell. They listened to a passionate plea from Ibrox chairman Rae Simpson, outlining why the club felt this was a grave injustice, and why the committee's assertion that the pitch invasion was an attempt to influence the result was an incorrect conclusion. The committee voted 23 to 15 to uphold the original decision to replay the match, a narrower vote than many had expected. It would now go to the Scottish League for ratification later in the week, with most insiders predicting that the league would not want to start a precedent of replaying matches, and a financial punishment would be the most likely final outcome.

It still meant the possibility of Rangers losing two points in the narrowest of championship tussles, and it still meant the club harboured a deep sense of injustice at how the SFA had handled the whole affair. Simpson went as far as calling it 'prejudged'. With Simpson a member of the league committee tasked with dealing with the SFA decision, there looked to be more fireworks ahead.

Ayr came calling at Ibrox on the Wednesday night, with their manager Alex Stuart attempting to deflect from his side's weekend drubbing by declaring to the press, 'The pressure is all on Rangers.' He backed up this claim by suggesting that his side had been the better team for half an hour, and would be a match for Rangers if they could maintain that level of performance for 90 minutes. Unusually, Jock Wallace seemed to abandon the routine philosophy of one game at a time. He stated, 'We are six wins from winning our second treble in three seasons. That's not bad, is it?'

Rangers v Ayr United
Wednesday, 12 April 1978, Ibrox
Peter McCloy, Sandy Jardine, John Greig, Tom Forsyth, Colin Jackson, Alex MacDonald, Tommy McLean, Bobby Russell, Derek Johnstone, Gordon Smith, Davie Cooper
Substitutes: Derek Parlane, Alex Miller

Glasgow hosted two hugely important games – but neither saw a crowd worthy of the occasion. While Aberdeen were beating Partick Thistle 4-2 at Hampden in the Scottish Cup semi-final in front just over 12,000 spectators, Ibrox also saw vast empty spaces and an almost identical attendance figure. It was no surprise that Rangers were unchanged, and the early stages suggested another rout was on the cards.

John Greig went close to scoring in a third successive match in just the fourth minute, then Derek Johnstone went even closer 13 minutes later when he unleashed a spectacular shot that crashed off the post with Hugh Sproat beaten. Two minutes later, the inevitable happened, with the scorer somewhat inevitable too. Davie Cooper slid an accurate pass to Johnstone, and the centre-forward sidestepped his marker before arrowing a low drive into the bottom corner.

APRIL: A CAPTAIN'S TALE

The small crowd were in good voice, knowing two more unanswered goals would see their team back on top of the league. In the 26th minute it looked like the first of these goals would arrive after Sandy Jardine was tripped in the penalty box by midfielder Gordon Crammond, referee Eddie Pringle having no option but to award the penalty. Cooper had scored with his previous spot-kick in the Scottish Cup win over Kilmarnock, and he was given the task of making the score 2-0. He struck the kick well but too close to Sproat, the goalkeeper making an excellent save then seeing Gordon Smith hit the side-netting with the rebound.

Within ten minutes the scoreline that should have read 2-0 was instead showing 1-1. The centre of the Rangers defence looked slow to react to a cross, and there was Gerry Phillips to stun the home crowd with a thumping header that flew past McCloy. With half-time approaching, Rangers piled forward to look to regain their lead, and Jackson was unlucky not to get on the scoresheet when he met a McLean corner perfectly only to see the ball hit a defender on the line, cannon on to the crossbar, then land in the arms of Sproat.

Pringle ended the first half with few in attendance able to believe that Rangers weren't comfortably ahead. Wallace must have run out of patience soon after the second half started, as he made a double change in the 50th minute when Derek Parlane and Alex Miller replaced Russell and McLean. This looked like a sign that Rangers were going more direct, with two of the more cultured players sacrificed.

There then followed a half-hour period that must have ranked as the most frustrating of the season so far. The Ayr goal seemed to have some kind of jinx over the ball as chance after chance went begging. The woodwork was struck twice more, taking the total to four in the match. Jackson was again the man to be denied when his header hit the outside of the post, then Jardine saw his beautifully struck 20-yard shot also smash off the upright. When they did get the ball on target, Rangers found Sproat in inspired form, and somehow the score remained at 1-1 until the final whistle.

The first of the two games in hand had been played, and Rangers still trailed by a point with a marginally inferior goal difference. It was difficult for Wallace to be too hard on his players, after a match that saw a missed penalty and the woodwork struck with such incredible regularity. 'It was one of those nights,' he said. 'We have four more league games and it's up to us to win them all.' The next match would be at Kilbowie against already-doomed Clydebank, just 24 hours before a 65,000 Ibrox sell-out to honour John Greig in his testimonial.

Aberdeen boss Billy McNeill, the long-time adversary of Greig when he was Celtic captain, showed that winning the title was more important than the friendship between the two Glasgow football legends when he withdrew his players Joe Harper, Willie Miller and Stuart Kennedy from the Scotland squad to play against Rangers in the testimonial. It was a decision that was viewed as pragmatic by those inside Ibrox, and they understood the reasoning behind it.

Meanwhile, as expected, the Scottish League committee charged with deciding whether to accept the SFA recommendation to replay the Motherwell v Rangers match at Fir Park refused to sanction another match, and instead asked the SFA to reconsider alternative punishments. Willie Waddell looked to be winning the day, although the next meeting of the SFA panel wasn't until the following week.

The weekend of Greig's testimonial arrived, but first of all there was the small matter of the closest title race in years to focus on. Wallace kept faith in the team who had somehow dropped a point in midweek, the only change coming on the bench where defender Alex Miller was replaced by the more positive Johnny Hamilton.

Clydebank v Rangers
Saturday, 15 April 1978, Kilbowie Park
Peter McCloy, Sandy Jardine, John Greig, Tom Forsyth, Colin Jackson, Alex MacDonald, Tommy McLean, Bobby Russell, Derek Johnstone, Gordon Smith, Davie Cooper
Substitutes: Derek Parlane, Johnny Hamilton

An all-ticket crowd of 9,800 packed into Kilbowie as season 1977/78 headed toward its conclusion. There were just two more Saturday rounds of fixtures to play, with Rangers also having a midweek match at Tannadice to come. That game was viewed by many as potentially the crucial 90 minutes remaining for Rangers, as they had two home games to finish off the campaign thereafter against Dundee United (again) and Motherwell. The game in hand represented the chance to overtake Aberdeen on points and put the title into their own hands.

But that was ignoring the challenge of Clydebank, who despite their league position were a good footballing team on their day, and they had recently beaten Celtic 3-2 on their tight little pitch.

The match started as mainly a midfield battle with chances few and far between. Again, Rangers seemed tentative, and it took the expert defending of Tom Forsyth to mop up a couple of dangerous Clydebank raids on the visiting goal. With Aberdeen at home to a Motherwell side who had little to play for other than a slight hope of European football for 1978/79, many in the ground started to feel that familiar frustration as time ticked on without any sign of a breakthrough.

Half chances for Smith and Cooper apart, it was a dull first half for the fans to endure and their mood hardly improved when the news from Pittodrie arrived that Aberdeen were already 4-0 in front. The goal-difference gap had widened, and with so few matches still to play it was looking as if a dropped point here could be fatal.

The nerves on the terraces did little to relax Rangers, but the tension was released ten minutes into the second half with the simplest of goals. The home defence made the fatal mistake of leaving Johnstone completely unmarked, and when the deadliest striker in the country got on the end of a cross just six yards out he was never going to miss with a simple header. It was goal number 34 of an amazing season for Johnstone, and when the game was finally put to bed in the closing ten minutes his total had reached 35. It was another relatively straightforward finish, low past Jim Gallacher from close range, and the sigh of relief from the Rangers fans could almost have been heard up in Aberdeen.

The match ended 2-0, but with their title rivals thrashing Motherwell 5-0, it was obvious that the most critical week of the entire campaign had arrived. Anything other than a win at Tannadice in midweek meant Aberdeen would be ahead with just two games to play, but a Rangers win would guarantee they had the destiny of the league flag in their own hands.

For the next 24 hours, however, thoughts of the crunch games to come were put aside. It was time to honour one of the greatest players to wear the Rangers shirt, with John Greig's testimonial match against a Scotland XI the chance for 65,000 fans to acclaim a man who had been a giant for the club on and off the park for the best part of two decades. It was a mark of the respect held among the support for their captain that the attendance was bigger than for any competitive fixture Rangers played in the entire season.

There was a scare before the match, however, as three Manchester United players got caught in the heavy traffic which had ground to a halt trying to reach Ibrox. Joe Jordan, Gordon McQueen and former Celtic man Lou Macari looked as if they wouldn't get to the stadium in time for kick-off, meaning some frantic rearranging of the team line-ups was required. Both Tom Forsyth and Derek Johnstone were dispatched to the away dressing room so that the Scotland team would muster 11 players, meaning Jock Wallace had to make changes to the side he wanted to play, his intention being to play his strongest 11 both in honour of Greig and also in preparation for Tannadice.

Luckily, after the intervention of a police escort, the Anglo-Scots made it to Ibrox in time, although it did mean a 20-minute delay to the kick-off. The crowd were entertained during this unplanned hold-up by comedian Andy Cameron, whose World Cup record was still in the charts, and who was a lifelong Rangers supporter. Forsyth and Johnstone changed back into their royal blue shirts, and the stage was finally set.

Rangers v Scotland XI
Sunday, 16 April 1978, Ibrox
Peter McCloy, Sandy Jardine, John Greig, Tom Forsyth, Colin Jackson, Alex MacDonald, Tommy McLean, Bobby Russell, Derek Johnstone, Gordon Smith, Davie Cooper
Substitutes: Derek Strickland, Kenny Watson

The Scotland team was a mixture of home-based players and star names from down south who were regulars in the national side. With Scotland boss Ally McLeod in charge, it was being treated as a warm-up match for the international team as they got ready to make the journey to Argentina, where both the manager and the Tartan Army were confident of going far in the tournament.

McLeod's team was: Jim Blyth (Coventry City), John Brownlie (Hibs), Brian Whittaker (Partick Thistle), Don Masson (Derby County), Gordon McQueen (Manchester United), Bruce Rioch (Derby County), John Robertson (Nottingham Forest), Ian Wallace (Coventry City), Joe Jordan (Manchester United), Asa Hartford (Manchester City), Archie Gemmill (Nottingham Forest). Lou Macari (Manchester United) was the substitute.

After a guard of honour from both teams for Greig, the match kicked off with Rangers on the attack straight away. And within 60 seconds the huge crowd had a goal to celebrate. It might have been Greig's special day, but there was nothing unique about the goalscorer or how he scored it – Johnstone outjumping McQueen to send a precise header past Jim Blyth and into the corner of the net. The goalkeeper would likely feel he could have done better to keep it out, while the Manchester United defender must have regretted the police getting him to Ibrox at all!

That set the tone for the first half in a match where those in blue appeared to be taking it a lot more seriously than the Scottish team in white. The Scots had a first-choice midfield on view, but the much-heralded Masson, Rioch and Hartford were outshone by young Bobby Russell, who stood out from the rest with his vision and positional sense. He sprayed passes right and left, and had the visitors chasing shadows. McLeod must have been relieved there were no more goals by the time referee Ian Foote ended the first half, whereas Wallace would have been delighted to see his team play so well with the season's finale ahead.

He was forced into a half-time change, however, Kenny Watson replacing Alex MacDonald who complained of feeling unwell when he got back into the dressing room. There was one other change made, Tommy McLean given 45 minutes' rest to allow the big crowd a glimpse of one of the promising youngsters from the successful Ibrox reserve team. Derek Strickland took to the field at the age of just 18 and acquitted himself well against such stellar opponents.

The changes didn't affect the flow of the match and fact Rangers dominated even more after the interval. Blyth did his chances of playing in Argentina no harm at all with some excellent stops, but even goalkeeping excellence wasn't going to deny Rangers on this big day. Right on the hour the moment came that 65,000 had been waiting for. Russell threaded a perfect pass to release the overlapping Jardine down the right, and his low cross found the unmarked Greig at the far post to knock the ball into the net from two yards out. The skipper milked the applause from his adoring public, and from that moment on the game was just a case of how many Rangers would score.

The answer to that question was five. Just three minutes after Greig's goal had brought the house down, Jardine played another killer pass, this time finding Russell in space just inside the Scottish penalty area. The midfielder took one touch to control it then lashed a brilliant shot past Blyth. It was a goal his display had deserved, but the number eight wasn't finished. In the 74th minute Watson played Russell through on goal and he casually flicked the ball past the advancing Blyth and into the net for Rangers' fourth. The Scotland players looked like they couldn't wait to hear the final whistle, but there was one more moment of misery for them yet. It was total joy for everyone else in the stadium.

With ten minutes left, Greig found himself back in the opposition penalty box, and when the ball fell to him 15 yards out he thumped it past Blyth to round off the scoring and to give the fans another excuse to ring his name all round Ibrox. The 5-0 scoreline was an embarrassing one for Scotland, although only their players would know just how seriously they took the match. Greig was swamped by team-mates and opponents alike at full time and the first testimonial match in over 50 years at Ibrox had been a resounding success. Ticket prices were the same as for a league match, meaning Greig made a British record £75,000 from the day, although money was a secondary consideration when compared to the massive outpouring of love for a man regarded as possibly the greatest of all the captains at a club that had seen many legendary skippers over the years.

The evening was completed with a dinner at the Ballochmyle restaurant in the city, the Scotland team all attending and presenting Greig with a gift of their own as a mark of their respect. The press reports the next day lavished praise on star man Russell, with several asking why he wasn't in the provisional squad for Argentina when he could so comprehensively outplay Scotland's best midfielders.

With the salute to the team captain now over, focus returned to the title race and the crucial midweek game in hand away to Dundee United. Red-hot goalscorer Derek Johnstone received another boost on the Monday afternoon when it was confirmed he had won the prestigious Scottish Football Writers' Player of the Year award, his 35 competitive goals so far making him the runaway choice. Johnstone became the fourth Rangers player in seven seasons to win the award, after Dave Smith in 1972, Jardine in 1975 and Greig in 1976. Johnstone would receive his award at a dinner on 1 May, which would be attended by prime minister James Callaghan, and the striker said, 'It is a tremendous honour to follow such great players who have won the award in the past ... it's one of the nicest things that has ever happened to me.'

The following day, the saga of the Motherwell v Rangers match finally ended with the news that the SFA Referees Committee had set aside their decision to replay the match, with a £2,000 fine imposed on Rangers instead. With this matter finally closed, all that mattered now was winning the remaining games and clinching a treble.

Alex MacDonald, such a key player in the side, failed to recover from illness and was ruled out of the trip to Tannadice. This would be the last time Rangers played outside of Glasgow in the season, with the two remaining league fixtures at Ibrox before the season finale at Hampden for the Scottish Cup Final. Jock Wallace declared the match 'a must-win', with opposing boss Jim McLean openly speaking of his desire to avenge the recent Scottish Cup loss. 'We played Rangers off the park for 70 minutes at Hampden,' he declared, 'now we want revenge.'

Dundee United v Rangers
Wednesday, 19 April 1978, Tannadice Park
Peter McCloy, Sandy Jardine, John Greig, Tom Forsyth, Colin Jackson, Kenny Watson, Tommy McLean, Bobby Russell, Derek Johnstone, Gordon Smith, Davie Cooper
Substitutes: Derek Parlane, Alex Miller

After impressing in his second-half showing in the Sunday testimonial match, it was Aberdonian midfielder Kenny Watson who was given the nod to replace MacDonald. With a win the only result that would take Rangers above his hometown club, there was a cup-tie atmosphere inside Tannadice, with both sets of fans in the 18,000 crowd in full voice as the teams took to the pitch. Maybe it was the occasion, maybe the atmosphere, or maybe the talk of revenge. Whatever the reason, the game soon degenerated into more of a battle than a football match.

The tone was set in the first few minutes when Tom Forsyth was left in a heap after a late tackle by Paul Sturrock, and for much of the remaining 85 minutes referee Hugh Alexander needed eyes in the back of his head to see the various feuds that had developed. Despite their reputation as a young and stylish footballing team, United had decided their best bet to beat Rangers was to go toe-to-toe and fight it out. With the massive experience, and the not inconsiderable physical presence of the Rangers defence, this seemed a strange approach. Forsyth revelled in the battle, and alongside John Greig, Colin Jackson and Sandy Jardine, the back four superbly marshalled the United attackers and prevented them from mustering a single meaningful effort on Peter McCloy's goal.

Alexander's patience was being tested, and eventually he booked both Frank Kopel and Paul Hegarty in the first half. And in among the blood and thunder there was also a goal. Just after a quarter of an hour, Greig moved forward and sent in a perfect cross. United goalkeeper Hamish McAlpine thought he could rush out to intercept it but he was beaten to the jump by the imperious Johnstone, and the ball was destined for the United net as soon as it left the head of Scotland's Player of the Year.

The huge Rangers travelling support hailed their heroes as they left the field for the interval, with the first chants of 'We're going to win the league' being heard for some time. There was still another 45 minutes of full commitment needed first, though, as United persisted with their aggressive approach in the second half. Perhaps the one moment that summed up the second half took place in the 62nd minute, as United were bringing on substitute David Dodds. Few in the ground saw what had happened but all of a sudden Sturrock was picking himself up off the turf and rubbing his jaw. It may not have been coincidence that the nearest player to him was Forsyth. 'Jaws' had bitten back!

Forsyth ended up being booked later on for hauling down Graham Payne, as did United's John Holt for a foul on the Rangers and Scotland defender. Alexander also had to give the United manager a stern lecture on the touchline when McLean had hurled abuse in his direction after a decision went Rangers' way. But as United grew increasingly frustrated, Rangers kept an iron grip on proceedings, seeing the match out with maximum efficiency and minimal scares. The final whistle sounded and the eruption of joy from the 10,000 Rangers supporters told the story. The team were back on top of the table with a one-point lead, and with just two home games left to play.

The manager was ecstatic, and determined this hard-fought win would build the platform for title glory. 'We are in front again, and we will stay there,' Wallace declared. 'If we win our last two matches the championship is ours. I'm confident my players won't let anybody down.'

Jim McLean was less than sporting in defeat. He moaned, 'My forwards were diabolical. There will definitely be changes for the trip to Ibrox on Saturday.' After such a feisty encounter with bad blood between some players, the teams playing each other again so quickly prompted fears of vendettas continuing and Rangers taking their eye off the main prize. We would know in just three days whether those fears were justified.

Rangers v Dundee United
Saturday, 22 April 1978, Ibrox
Peter McCloy, Sandy Jardine, John Greig, Tom Forsyth, Colin Jackson, Alex MacDonald, Tommy McLean, Bobby Russell, Derek Johnstone, Gordon Smith, Davie Cooper
Substitutes: Derek Parlane, Kenny Watson

Alex MacDonald was passed fit on the morning of the match, and his return allowed Jock Wallace to name the 11 regarded widely as his strongest available. The club decided that with the title now in sight they would add some extra entertainment to the occasion with music played on the pitch both before kick-off and at half-time by the massed bands of the Glasgow Boys' Brigade. There was the possibility of clinching a 37th Scottish title on the day, if Rangers won and Aberdeen slipped to defeat at Pittodrie against St Mirren. Over 27,000 inside Ibrox hoped that might be how things worked out.

From the first minute, it was clear that this would be a very different game from midweek. With MacDonald's energy and ball winning combined with Bobby Russell's calm passing, Rangers took control of the midfield. They had already tested Hamish McAlpine before taking the lead in just the fourth minute. Tommy McLean chipped in a free kick that was yet again met by the head of Johnstone and most inside the ground, including McAlpine, would have expected the deadly striker to nod the ball in for a goal. Instead Johnstone head flicked the ball across the goal where Colin Jackson was in space. The big centre-half didn't connect cleanly but succeeded in bundling the ball over the line from close range.

An early goal was exactly what Rangers had been hoping for, and with the crowd roaring them on they went for more.

Johnstone was giving the United defenders a torrid time and on 20 minutes his power and persistence gave Rangers the perfect opportunity to make it 2-0. He took possession outside the United penalty box and strode forward, holding off defender Ray Stewart. The full-back rashly dived in, and clattered the striker to the ground inside the area for a blatant penalty. Sandy Jardine took the kick and easily beat McAlpine. The celebrations of the players showed how much it meant, and from that moment on there was never any doubt where the points were heading.

United, who had dropped Paul Sturrock to the bench after his unusually physical midweek display, were toothless in attack on the rare occasions they got forward, with Tom Forsyth in particular dealing easily with any potential threat. The match coasted to half-time with Rangers totally dominant, and many of the crowd were now wondering more about the score at Aberdeen than worrying about the destiny of the points at Ibrox. The excitement levels grew when the news reached Govan that St Mirren held a 2-1 lead after 45 minutes.

When referee Bill Anderson got things under way again, the second half settled into a pattern of Rangers dominance after a short initial flurry of pressure from United that found the Ibrox defence in impenetrable form. The home team gradually took control again once United's enthusiasm waned, but without any great urgency to add to the scoreline. Then out of the blue Rangers scored a magnificent third goal with 16 minutes left. MacDonald showed brilliant close control to beat his opposite number Bobby Robinson before chipping a delightful through ball into the path of Davie Cooper. The winger let fly first time with a scorching shot from the edge of the area that simply flew past McAlpine before the goalkeeper could move.

It was a goal fit to win a title, but Aberdeen had mounted a comeback in their match, and their 4-2 win meant any celebrations were on hold for another week. With one game left for each team, Rangers were on 51 points and that precious single point in front. Rangers were overwhelming favourites now to be champions, their final fixture being at home to an off-form Motherwell, but with a superior goal difference Aberdeen hadn't given up hope. They knew that even a draw at Ibrox would mean their first title since 1955 if they won at Easter Road, and only the second league championship win in their history.

Jock Wallace was a confident man. He simply stated that at the start of the season that he would have been delighted to have a home match on the final day with the title guaranteed with a win. His week started with some transfer business, however, the club accepting a £30,000 offer for striker Martin Henderson from Philadelphia Furies of the North American Soccer League. Henderson, who had been a key man in the last treble season under Wallace in 1975/76, had failed to dislodge Johnstone and Derek Parlane as the first-choice centre-forwards, and had spent most of the season on loan at Hibs.

There were also two reserve matches played within 24 hours of each other that allowed Wallace to give some game time to his fringe players, with Parlane, Alex Miller and Kenny Watson all playing in both victories over Partick Thistle and Celtic. Parlane in particular impressed, scoring the winner at Parkhead in the Reserve League clash. The end of the week was entirely focused on preparation for the title decider. The manager gave a rallying call to the fans, asking for them to turn out in big numbers and roar the team to glory. 'We want their encouragement from the first kick of the ball,' he said. 'The championship is now there for us.'

APRIL: A CAPTAIN'S TALE

With no injury concerns after the impressive dismantling of Dundee United, an unchanged team was regarded as a certainty. One player who would definitely not be forcing his way back into the line-up was Johnny Hamilton, a hero of the League Cup Final win over Celtic in March. Rangers made the surprise announcement just 48 hours before kick-off that he had been given a free transfer, and the popular midfielder had played his last game for the club. Hamilton seemed quite happy with this, saying, 'In a way, it's a bit of a relief. I've had five happy years at Ibrox ... but with the club having so much midfield talent at their disposal I feel that it's the right time to move on.'

Another player given a free transfer was legendary striker Colin Stein, who had just completed a loan with Kilmarnock. The hero of Barcelona in 1972, and the man who scored the goal in 1975 that brought back the league title after an 11-year wait, had his place in the Ibrox hall of fame secured long ago. As well as those leaving the club, Wallace also confirmed that goalkeeper Stewart Kennedy was on the transfer list. The big Stirling-born stopper had been the number one for a large part of the season, and the player expressed his massive disappointment at the decision that he was no longer in the manager's plans.

Many expressed some surprise at these announcements being made before the season had ended, but with the players now aware of their futures, Wallace and his team now could concentrate on clinching their third league flag in four seasons.

Rangers v Motherwell
Saturday, 29 April 1978, Ibrox
Peter McCloy, Sandy Jardine, John Greig, Tom Forsyth, Colin Jackson, Alex MacDonald,

Tommy McLean, Bobby Russell, Derek Johnstone, Gordon Smith, Davie Cooper
Substitutes: Derek Parlane, Kenny Watson

The attendance given out after the match was just under 47,000, although most present thought that there seemed more in the ground. It certainly sounded a lot closer to a full house when the team took the field to a huge roar. As expected, Wallace had given a vote of confidence to the same 11 and substitutes as the previous week, and they again went straight on the attack as soon as referee Tommy Muirhead blew the opening whistle.

That roar got even louder when the early goal Rangers craved arrived after just six minutes. Motherwell, who fielded a team composed of experience and youth, conceded a free kick on Rangers' left some 40 yards from goal when Willie Watson flattened Cooper. Greig launched the ball high into the Motherwell box, and up jumped Johnstone and Jackson alongside a Motherwell defender. It was Jackson who climbed highest, and he connected with a firm and accurate header that found the far corner of the net past a well-beaten Stuart Rennie.

The party had started and Rangers were in no mood to allow it to be spoiled. With Bobby Russell again outstanding in the middle of the park, they laid siege on the Motherwell goal, knowing one more would surely kill off the game and win the championship. They did have Peter McCloy to thank, however, on 11 minutes when Stewart McLaren got on the end of a swift counterattack and hit a low shot from 12 yards.

But at the other end Rennie was having a busier afternoon, and in the 19th minute the ball was in his net again. The goal was all down to Johnstone, who showed what a fine footballer he was and not just deadly in the air.

APRIL: A CAPTAIN'S TALE

He took a pass in the inside-left channel, drove into the area, beat his defender with some neat footwork, then hit a low cross from the goal line. Rennie tried to stop the ball at his near post but succeeded only in deflecting it across his empty goal, and there was the predatory Gordon Smith to gleefully tuck the ball into the open net from five yards. Smith and his team-mates celebrated as if they knew that was the title won.

Perhaps they briefly lost concentration as four minutes later there was a lucky escape when Tom Forsyth appeared to catch youngster Jim Lindsay in the Rangers penalty box, but as 47,000 fans held their breath Muirhead signalled that the visiting player had dived. That was to be as close as Motherwell would come all afternoon to upsetting the odds. By half-time Rangers could have been another two goals in front. First, Alex MacDonald smashed a shot off the crossbar with Rennie well beaten, then Johnstone almost grabbed his customary goal but missed the target by inches with another thumping strike.

A 2-0 lead at the break was totally acceptable, however, the fans using the half-time break to practice their songs of celebration for the expected party. The second half saw Rangers play a more containing game, and as the visitors were allowed a greater share of possession they did fashion a couple of half chances that were snuffed out by more good McCloy goalkeeping. The best chance of the half fell to goalscorer Smith on the hour, but he first hit the post and then struck Rennie with the rebound.

As the game entered injury time, the fans had already started chants of triumph, and Rangers forced a corner. John Greig stood over the ball as the referee ran across to him, picked up the ball and signalled that the game had ended. It was fitting that Greig was the man who raised his arms aloft in triumph, as the first player made aware it was full-time. Wallace rushed on to the pitch, as was his custom after a trophy win. Every player was given a hug by the manager, with a special smile kept for his embrace with his captain. Greig was carried shoulder-high by his team-mates, as the tannoy played 'Congratulations' by Cliff Richard. Most of the songs sung on the terraces would never be part of his pop repertoire!

As the champagne corks popped, Wallace spoke of his delight, and his unshakable belief in this group of players. 'I never had any doubts we would do it,' he said. 'I'm also delighted to get another chance at the European Cup. We weren't ready for Europe last September with Cooper, Russell and Smith never having experienced it before. But if we can play as we can next season, we will take a bit of stopping. We now look forward to the Scottish Cup Final and the chance to win a second treble in three seasons. That's not bad going, is it?'

The eventual winning margin was two points as Aberdeen closed out their season with a draw at Easter Road. Without their challenge, Rangers would have sewn up the title long ago.

April ended in triumph for Rangers and with just the one game to come in the new month against the team who had run them so close. It was a match that could earn the team of 1977/78 immortality.

11

May: Treble Glory Then the End of an Era

WITH THE title now safely secured, Jock Wallace decided on full training at the start of the week leading up to the Scottish Cup Final, with final preparations during a training camp near Largs. On the Monday night, Derek Johnstone received his Scottish Football Writers' Player of the Year award at a dinner at Glasgow's Albany Hotel. But it was an event the following day that had the attention of the Rangers players, management and supporters. It was the latest meeting of the SFA Referees Committee, a body who had been very much in conflict with the club in the very recent past. This time they were to decide on suitable disciplinary punishments for several players across many clubs, but two cases in particular were of Ibrox interest.

Derek Parlane faced a suspension for his dismissal against Hibs at Easter Road at the end of March, a decision that Wallace at the time angrily denounced. The other Rangers player in the dock was Alex MacDonald, who was appealing against a fourth booking. Should his appeal be dismissed then he would also face a ban. As the cup final was the last match of the season in Scotland, the timing of the meeting meant that any Rangers player suspended would miss the Hampden date, whereas players from any other team would not miss a match of the current campaign but instead start the following one on the sidelines. Many in football were watching closely for the outcome, with Rangers fans feeling that this particular committee were biased against the club after their earlier decision to replay the Motherwell league game. Meanwhile, Aberdeen fans were hoping to see a couple of Rangers stars ruled out of the big game against their side.

Both players showed how important the outcome was to them by appearing in person, and in the end the result was 1-1, with Rangers winning one and losing one case. Parlane had his appeal against his red card dismissed, and was given a four-day suspension starting from the following morning, plus a one-match ban at the start of season 1978/79. This meant he was ruled out of the final but could play in any replay. MacDonald, however, was cleared to play at Hampden after his appeal was accepted.

The manager took the news with a mixture of relief and frustration. 'I am pleased for Alex, but naturally very disappointed for Derek,' Wallace said simply. He wouldn't make any comment on the other contentious decision of the committee, who decided on a £1,000 fine for Celtic after a pitch invasion by their fans in a defeat at Easter Road. This was half of the fine Rangers received for the same offence by their supporters at Motherwell, despite the cases looking to be very similar. Aberdeen ended up in a similar position to Rangers in that they also had a player banned for the final, defender Doug Rougvie given a similar punishment to Parlane. Like the Rangers man, he was expected to be a substitute at best for the match.

MAY: TREBLE GLORY THEN THE END OF AN ERA

On the Wednesday, Ally McLeod confirmed his 22-man squad for the World Cup. There were few surprises, with three Rangers stars long assured of their place on the plane to South America. Sandy Jardine, Tom Forsyth and Derek Johnstone all hoped to play a significant part in Scotland's effort to conquer the football world.

The focus was now fully on Hampden, and although the bookmakers made the new champions favourites to complete the clean sweep, it wasn't lost on Wallace or the Rangers fans that Aberdeen were in a rich vein of form. They were on an unbeaten run that now stretched back 23 matches, and had won their last three meetings with Rangers by the incredible aggregate score of 10-1. Punters could get odds of 2/1 on an Aberdeen win, with Rangers the 5/4 favourites.

Rangers headed to the Ayrshire coast and added striker Chris Robertson to the travelling party of 16 players in place of Parlane. Robertson was set to create an unusual piece of football trivia, having come on as a substitute in the 1977 final then hardly played since apart from a brief spell in the team at the start of the campaign when other forwards were unavailable. As Rangers relaxed in their Largs headquarters, Aberdeen travelled south to base themselves in a Glasgow hotel. Both managers were confident but respectful of the opposition.

'We are here to win,' stated Wallace. 'It should be a tremendous match, both teams have shown what they can do throughout the season.' His counterpart Billy McNeill said, 'Neither team has anything to hide from the other. It's a case of whoever plays better on the day will win.'

Rangers v Aberdeen
Saturday, 6 May 1978, Hampden
Peter McCloy, Sandy Jardine, John Greig,

Tom Forsyth, Colin Jackson, Alex MacDonald, Tommy McLean, Bobby Russell, Derek Johnstone, Gordon Smith, Davie Cooper
Substitutes: Kenny Watson, Chris Robertson

The 61,563 attendance was the largest of the Scottish domestic season, although remarkably it was almost 3,500 fewer than had turned out to honour John Greig at his testimonial. The Aberdeen fans flocked to the national stadium in confident mood, their team's form against Rangers giving them real cause for optimism. The pundits were split on who was most likely to lift the trophy, and in one newspaper it seemed the other managers in the league were equally divided. Bill Munro of Clydebank and Benny Rooney of newly promoted Morton both took Aberdeen, while Willie Ormond of Hearts and Alex Ferguson of St Mirren plumped for Rangers. As far as Jim McLean of Dundee United and Bertie Auld of Partick Thistle were concerned, it was too close to call.

The teams were led out by captains at very different stages of their careers on a sunny day in Mount Florida. John Greig at 35 years of age was looking to add a sixth Scottish Cup winners' medal to his enormous collection, whereas 22-year-old Willie Miller was playing in his first Scottish Cup Final. Both teams were introduced to the retiring SFA president Rankin Grimshaw, and then at last battle could commence.

It was Aberdeen who seemed to settle the quicker, and they created the first good chance inside three minutes. John McMaster was lurking with menace just outside the Rangers penalty box, and when the ball was laid into his path he hit a ferocious shot that whistled just over the bar with Peter McCloy nowhere near it. Rangers hit back with a short spell of pressure of their own, Alex MacDonald shooting over four minutes later from a promising position before Gordon Smith's effort then did hit the target but lacked the power to worry Bobby Clark.

Gradually Rangers were taking control, and it was in no small part down to a couple of tactical adjustments made by Wallace after the pain of the last two heavy defeats to the men in red. Aberdeen had used their numerical advantage in midfield and the overlapping runs of their full-backs to great effect in those victories, the manager adopting a different shape to his side this time. Gordon Smith played a slightly deeper role, giving Rangers an extra man in the middle of the park when Aberdeen got possession, and making it harder for them to get the space to pick a pass. Then there was the disciplined performance of winger Davie Cooper, who was tracking the runs of the dangerous Dons right-back Stuart Kennedy, and nullifying his threat on the outside.

This all allowed Bobby Russell to get more time on the ball than he had enjoyed in recent tussles with Aberdeen, and the youngster was making the most of it. He gradually began running the show, the heartbeat of the team in the engine room, complemented in there by Smith's clever positional awareness and the energy and ball winning of the non-stop MacDonald. Aberdeen were slowly beginning to lose their way but they remained dangerous on the rare occasions they did get themselves within sight of goal, Drew Jarvie trying a shot from distance that flew narrowly over.

But it was Russell who was stamping his class on proceedings, and he drew cheers from the massive Rangers following midway through the half when he looked hemmed in near his own penalty box by Jarvie, but escaped from the forward with a clever shimmy and an accurate forward pass. Rangers broke upfield and forced a corner which saw

Colin Jackson rise to meet the ball but he couldn't keep his header down.

The slim number eight was at the centre of everything good Rangers were doing, and in the 35th minute Russell unlocked the Aberdeen defence to set up the crucial opening goal. Smith and Cooper started the move, and the ball found its way to Derek Johnstone some 20 yards out with his back to goal. The striker played the ball back to Russell on the right. The midfielder looked up and spotted a darting run from Alex MacDonald going in behind the Aberdeen central defenders. Russell produced an inch-perfect floated pass over the defence, and MacDonald dived full length to connect with a diving header. Goalkeeper Clark had started to come for the cross and dived too late to get there, the ball just squirming past his despairing hands.

The Rangers end was a sea of celebration, with big-game scorer MacDonald showing again what a knack he had in popping up when it mattered most. The successful appeal against his suspension was looking even more important now. Rangers saw out the remaining ten minutes of the half quite comfortably, the only half chances falling to Russell and Greig. When referee Brian McGinlay ended the first 45 minutes they were halfway to that dream treble.

There were no changes made by either manager at the interval, and if the Dons supporters expected to see their team go all out for an equaliser on the restart they were to be disappointed. Rangers retained their iron grip on things, the midfield battle now looking as if it had been won decisively. The play was all towards the Aberdeen goal, and eight minutes into the second half it should have been 2-0. Rangers won a corner and when it was played into the Aberdeen area, it fell to Cooper. His attempt was blocked by a desperate defender but broke perfectly for Tom Forsyth just a few yards out. Despite being the match winner in the cup final five years earlier, 'Jaws' was never particularly comfortable in front of goal, and his mishit shot proved that. Clark blocked the ball, and the chance was gone.

Billy McNeill had seen enough, and a few minutes later he took off the ineffectual Ian Fleming and gave recent signing Ian Scanlon his chance to become a Pittodrie hero. It made little difference, Rangers still powering forward, and on 61 minutes the goal that had been threatened duly arrived. Rangers won a throw-in on the right, in line with the Aberdeen 18-yard box. Tommy McLean took it short to Sandy Jardine, who returned the ball to the diminutive winger. Despite being tight on the touchline and being faced by two defenders, McLean shifted the ball quickly to get a yard of space and then flighted over a hanging cross. In the middle of the box waited Johnstone, and he rose majestically to bullet an unstoppable header into the far top corner from almost on the penalty spot. It was a scorer all the way, past Clark before he could even dive.

The wild jubilation on the Rangers terraces summed up what the fans, and the players, knew. It was game over. Johnstone had scored his 39th goal of a quite magnificent season, netting in his third different Scottish Cup Final. There was still half an hour for Aberdeen to mount a comeback but they looked a beaten team, heads down and helpless to stop the Ibrox juggernaut.

They did try to test the rock-solid Rangers rearguard, but the back four of Jardine, Forsyth, Jackson and Greig played like the experienced international players they were. Jarvie and Steve Ritchie had desperate attempts at goal, both well over Peter McCloy's crossbar, and the party was starting around three-quarters of Hampden. Wallace replaced the hard-working Cooper with the more defensive

Kenny Watson for the closing stages as extra insurance, and the match reached the 85th minute with Rangers coasting to victory. Then, out of the blue, they conceded a bizarre goal.

McMaster played a ball across the face of the penalty area but full-back Ritchie completely mistimed his shot from ten yards, the ball looping high into the air. McCloy assumed it was sailing over, and he swung on the crossbar after deciding not to attempt the save. To his horror, and to the absolute astonishment of everyone else inside Hampden, the ball dropped from the sky, over his shoulder and into the net. It took the Aberdeen players a few seconds to register they had scored, so unlikely it had all been. They *had* scored, and suddenly after cruising to the line, Rangers had five more minutes to survive.

But, despite this late lifeline, Aberdeen never looked like breaching the Rangers defence again. The 90 minutes passed, McCloy punted a trademark goal kick high up the field, and McGinlay blew his whistle to end the cup final. Rangers had done it, a record fourth treble had been won, and a second in just three seasons. As was his tradition, Wallace ran to his players out on the pitch with hugs all round.

After John Greig had held the old trophy aloft, the lap of honour seemed even more jubilant than usual; perhaps the players and fans all knew how close a battle it had been and what a rollercoaster the past weeks had become. As the players ran around the national stadium with the cup, Gordon Smith wearing the almost obligatory funny hat, this felt like a Rangers team who had asserted their domestic dominance and who had the perfect blend of youth and experience to continue that domination for some time yet.

After the match, Wallace took time to praise two men in particular, summing up perfectly that winning blend.

First, he spoke about the club captain, the 35-year old who had agreed a new contract to continue playing next season. 'Who can tell when John will quit?' he said. 'I certainly can't, and as long as he continues to play as he has, that suits me fine.' His next thoughts were about the young man of the match, Bobby Russell's name being on everyone's lips after an incredible first senior season, 'There's just no telling how far this boy can go in the game. His skill is uncanny, and perhaps just as important he remains completely unaffected by his success. He is a manager's dream.'

Wallace then made sure the rest of his team weren't forgotten. 'We hadn't a poor player,' he smiled. 'I took off Davie Cooper, but Coop had done well in a different role. How often did you see Stuart Kennedy raiding down the wing?'

No doubt the party continued long into the night, and the next evening Derek Johnstone had even more cause to celebrate. At the inaugural Scottish Players' Association awards, held in Glasgow, the country's top goalscorer added the Players' Player of the Year award to the one already received from the country's journalists. His 39 goals for the club had been a massive reason why Rangers were treble champions, and the big striker now had a World Cup to look forward to, with many in the press and in the Tartan Army clamouring for him to start up front.

In perhaps an indication of the differing expectations at both clubs, the Sunday also saw Billy McNeill and his Aberdeen players take part in an open-top bus parade through the streets of the city. Despite their season ending trophyless thanks to defeats in all competitions at the hands of their Ibrox rivals, the Dons fans turned out in good number to cheer their team and thank them for their efforts. An estimated 10,000 supporters lined the streets, with a further 10,000 or so inside Pittodrie for the final stage of their journey. McNeill thanked them, and said, 'We have made a resolution to give you a trophy next year.' A few days later, McNeill did win a prize when he was confirmed as the McKinlay's Personality of the Year, which won him the sum of £250 plus a very large bottle of whisky. He was also announced as Manager of the Year by a panel of sports writers, who had obviously decided on the award before the season had ended and now looked very foolish. Safe to say that Jock Wallace wouldn't have swapped any of his prizes for these!

With season 1977/78 now over, thoughts turned to international football with the upcoming British Home Championship series, and to the usual rumours and excitement of summer transfer activity. Those home international matches started with Johnstone scoring against Northern Ireland and Wales, and despite the games both ending 1-1 he had further cemented his claim as the hottest goalscorer available to Ally McLeod. The goal against Wales was by common consent in the press box one of the best headers ever scored at Hampden. Then, incredibly, he wasn't selected for the 1-0 defeat to England, and more incredibly he also never got a single minute on the pitch in Argentina as the Scots suffered ignominious failure. A stirring 3-2 win over the Netherlands in the final group game wasn't enough to salvage qualification after shambolic defeat to Peru and an embarrassing draw with Iran. To this day, it's never been fully explained why a man with 41 goals for club and country to his name over the season wasn't given any opportunity to fire his country to glory.

Sandy Jardine and Tom Forsyth did get to take part in football's biggest tournament, but if they were surprised at how the Scotland campaign unfolded, it was nothing to the shock they had already received on the evening of Tuesday, 23 May. Just 17 days after leading his side to a second treble in three seasons, Jock Wallace stunned the whole of Scottish football by resigning from the job he coveted most in the world. To a shocked group of reporters, club secretary Frank King read a prepared statement, 'The directors have to announce that Mr Jock Wallace has resigned as Rangers manager. His resignation has been accepted with regret. The board are grateful for all he has done for the club, and wish him well in his future career.'

There had been rumours circulating in Glasgow over the previous 48 hours that Leicester City, newly relegated to England's Second Division, were on the verge of confirming Wallace as their new manager, but few believed this was remotely possible; the man was Rangers to the core. Vice-chairman and general manager Willie Waddell refused to answer any questions posed to him by reporters, only telling the press to refer to the club statement. The whispers around the terraces that the two men did not see eye to eye were maybe now being confirmed, although neither would ever disclose their thoughts on the matter in public.

Supporters were stunned, a small group gathering at the stadium to hear for themselves the news that they refused to believe. It was also a massive blow to the players, most of whom were very much moulded in Wallace's beliefs of hard work, attractive football, will to win, physical fitness, and the overarching importance of the club. At just 42 years old Wallace left Ibrox as the first (and still the only at the time of publication) Rangers manager to win two trebles. He was indeed confirmed as the new Leicester boss within 48 hours of his departure, his heart undoubtedly still back in Govan. Just nine months after the fans chanting for his removal, his departure was a sad day for the entire Rangers support.

Speculation now started as to who would be tasked with the unenviable job of replacing Wallace in the Ibrox hot seat. Names like former player and St Mirren boss Alex Ferguson were mentioned along with Scotland manager Ally McLeod. But the Rangers board were in no doubt who the right man was, and the very next afternoon they asked captain John Greig to move from the dressing room to the manager's office. The club legend immediately accepted, and at the same time ended his 17-year playing career, all of it spent in the blue of Rangers. He admitted to a reporter, 'It will never be the same again,' which would turn out to be something of an understatement. The new boss added, 'I realise the size of the task facing me. It's the biggest managerial job in the country, but I think I'm helped by the fact I've been at Ibrox for so long as a player. I know just what is required of the manager.'

While Greig was being pictured with his wife and young son for the front pages of the morning editions, his former team-mate and good friend Derek Johnstone was sensationally handing in a transfer request, unsettled after multiple reports of interest in his signature from English giants Arsenal. He gave an interview to a Glasgow evening newspaper explaining his reasons, while also surprising readers by saying that any club seeking his signature would see him as a central defender as that was where he wanted to play.

This truly was the end of an era, and not just at Rangers. Greig would go on to persuade his star player to stay at the club after appointing Johnstone as the new captain, and he would enjoy success in both domestic cups and reach a European Cup quarter-final in his first season in the dugout. But he had the virtually impossible problem of replacing himself, as well as inheriting a team which had several battle-hardened men of huge experience who were passing the peak of their powers. Greig struggled to find the right blend, and never managed to win the league title in just over five seasons in charge.

Over at Parkhead, another huge change was under way with the removal of the legendary Jock Stein as manager to be replaced by Manager of the Year Billy McNeill, for so many years the club captain and the great friend and rival of Greig. One of the most famous rivalries in the history of the game would now move from the pitch to the touchlines. Both men would have to cope with a new challenge from further north, not just worry about each other. Season 1977/78 had seen Aberdeen emerge as a new force in the Scottish game, and when they appointed Alex Ferguson as McNeill's replacement, it heralded an age of unparalleled success for the club. Along with the challenge of Jim McLean's exciting Dundee United side after they started to fulfil their potential shown in the previous season, a 'New Firm' had appeared to take on the established power base. This new era in Scottish football would see multiple trophies, and European success, for teams outside of Glasgow.

At international level, the tidal wave of optimism prior to the Argentina debacle proved to be the undoing of Ally McLeod, his assertion that the Scottish football team was capable of winning a medal when competing with the world's best had been believed by too many for them to accept an early exit. From then on, no Scotland manager would ever be as upbeat, with pragmatism and 'accepting our place' becoming the mantra with successive bosses. There were still many big tournaments to play in, but never again would the country feel as good about its football team. The new realism was illustrated just four years later when an equally talented squad again suffered glorious failure and went home after the group stage. There was no national outcry, and no question of manager Jock Stein being replaced. Some might suggest that part of the joy of being a Scotland fan had been diluted.

There was one other major change off the pitch at Ibrox too. The old terraces were to become a thing of the past, Rangers announcing a complete revamp of Ibrox, converting it from the massive 65,000 capacity bowl into a modern seated stadium holding just over 40,000 when completed. Before the new season kicked off, the bulldozers arrived to flatten the traditional 'Rangers end' of Ibrox, with the Copland Road stand to be built during season 1978/79 before two other brand new stands were constructed in the following seasons. Willie Waddell's promise to the club, and to himself, that the horrors of 2 January 1971 would never happen again was being put into action.

Never again would Rangers fans see the vast home crowds of before, the swaying masses on the slopes of Ibrox celebrating together in one heaving mass. And gone also would be the tall and steep staircase exits, watching the match uncovered in the pouring rain, and the primitive toilet facilities. Rangers were leading the way in building a more modern Scottish football with the 'old days' drawing to a close. The cost of this upgrade was substantial, paid for mostly from the proceeds of the successful Rangers Pools operation, but it also meant that new manager Greig had the added handicap of playing big matches in a three-quarters stadium as well as money being initially tight for any incoming transfers.

Rangers' history shows the glorious success of season 1977/78. A treble, a refreshed team at the zenith of its powers, a captain and a manager who were adored. It was the peak year of a glorious Rangers era, but gave way quickly

MAY: TREBLE GLORY THEN THE END OF AN ERA

to a time of great change and little success. It would be nine frustrating seasons before the league title finally returned, the 'Souness Revolution' finally bringing back the glory years in that modernised Ibrox after the best efforts of that great captain, and then that great manager returning, but both failing to deliver the prize that will always be coveted most in Scottish football. And one of the stars of the team who delivered the title back to Ibrox was a man who made his debut for the club on the opening day of 1977/78, the late, great Davie Cooper. For him, this amazing campaign hadn't been an ending, it had been the start of an unforgettable career at the club he loved.

Season 1977/78 started with no trophies in the trophy room, and within two matches it saw fans call for the manager to be sacked. After it ended in magnificent success, it was followed by a long period of lows before glory finally returned. This chapter in the history of Scotland's most successful football club is perfectly summed up by the most famous quote from the greatest Rangers manager of them all, the immortal William Struth. What better way to end the story of the fourth of seven Rangers trebles:

'Never fear, inevitably we shall have our years of failure, and when they arrive, we must reveal tolerance and sanity. No matter the days of anxiety that come our way, we shall emerge stronger because of the trials to be overcome. That has been the philosophy of the Rangers since the days of the gallant pioneers.'

Appendix:
Full 1977/78 Competitive Results and Player Statistics

RESULTS

Date	Opposition	Venue	Comp	Result	Scorers
06/08/77	Southampton	H	TC	3-1	MacDonald, Parlane, Cooper
07/08/77	West Brom	H	TC	0-2	
13/08/77	Aberdeen	A	PD	1-3	Russell
17/08/77	Young Boys	H	ECWC	1-0	Greig
24/07/77	Hibs	H	PD	0-2	
24/08/77	St Johnstone	H	LC	3-1	Johnstone (2), Miller (pen)
27/08/77	Partick Thistle	A	PD	4-0	Miller (pen), Smith (2), Russell
31/08/77	Young Boys	A	ECWC	2-2	Johnstone, Smith
03/09/77	St Johnstone	A	LC	3-0	Parlane, Miller (pen), Smith
10/09/77	Celtic	H	PD	3-2	Smith (2), Johnstone
14/09/77	FC Twente	H	ECWC	0-0	
17/09/77	St Mirren	A	PD	3-3	Jardine, Cooper, Johnstone
24/09/77	Ayr United	H	PD	2-0	Smith (2)
28/09/77	FC Twente	A	ECWC	0-3	
01/10/77	Clydebank	H	PD	4-1	Cooper (2), Smith (2)
05/10/77	Aberdeen	H	LC	6-1	Smith (3), Johnstone, Miller (pen), MacDonald

FULL 1977/78 COMPETITIVE RESULTS AND PLAYER STATISTICS

08/10/77	Dundee United	A	PD	1-0	Russell
15/10/77	Motherwell	A	PD	4-1	Smith, Johnstone (3)
18/10/77	Partick Thistle	H	GC	2-2**	Forsyth, McLean
22/10/77	Aberdeen	H	PD	3-1	Jardine (pen), Smith, MacDonald
26/10/77	Aberdeen	A	LC	1-3	Smith
29/10/77	Hibs	A	PD	1-0	Jardine (pen)
05/11/77	Partick Thistle	H	PD	3-3	Parlane (2), MacDonald
09/11/77	Dunfermline	H	LC	3-1	Jackson, McLean (2)
12/11/77	Celtic	A	PD	1-1	Johnstone
16/11/77	Dunfermline	A	LC	3-1	Greig, Jardine (pen), Johnstone
19/11/77	St Mirren	H	PD	2-1	Johnstone, Miller (pen)
26/11/77	Ayr United	A	PD	5-0	Johnstone (3), Jackson, Parlane
10/12/77	Dundee United	H	PD	2-0	McLean, Smith
17/12/77	Motherwell	H	PD	3-1	Smith (2), Johnstone
24/12/77	Aberdeen	A	PD	0-4	
31/12/77	Hibs	H	PD	0-0	
02/01/78	Partick Thistle	A	PD	2-1	Johnstone, Smith
07/01/78	Celtic	H	PD	3-1	Smith, Greig, Parlane
14/01/78	St Mirren	A	PD	2-0	Johnstone, Smith
28/01/78	Berwick Rangers	A	SC	4-2	Jackson (2), Johnstone (2)
04/02/78	Clydebank	H	PD	1-0	Johnstone
18/02/78	Stirling Albion	H	SC	1-0	Johnstone
19/02/78	Clydebank	A	PD	3-0	Johnstone (2), Cooper
25/02/78	Motherwell	A	PD	5-3	Johnstone (2), Smith, Cooper, Own Goal

1977/78

Date	Opponent	Venue	Comp	Score	Scorers
27/02/78	Forfar	N	LC	5-2*	Johnstone (2), Parlane (2), MacDonald
04/03/78	Aberdeen	H	PD	0-3	
11/03/78	Kilmarnock	H	SC	4-1	Johnstone, Hamilton, MacDonald, Cooper (pen)
18/03/78	Celtic	N	LCF	2-1*	Cooper, Smith
21/03/78	Partick Thistle	H	PD	2-1	MacDonald, Jardine
25/03/78	Celtic	A	PD	0-2	
29/03/78	Hibs	A	PD	1-1	Parlane
01/04/78	St Mirren	H	PD	1-1	Johnstone
05/04/78	Dundee United	N	SC	2-0	Johnstone, Greig
08/04/78	Ayr United	A	PD	5-2	Johnstone (2), Greig, Smith (2)
12/04/78	Ayr United	H	PD	1-1	Johnstone
15/04/77	Clydebank	A	PD	2-0	Johnstone (2)
16/04/77	Scotland XI	H	TEST	5-0	Johnstone, Greig (2), Russell (2)
19/04/78	Dundee United	A	PD	1-0	Johnstone
22/04/78	Dundee United	H	PD	3-0	Jackson, Jardine (pen), Cooper
29/04/78	Motherwell	H	PD	2-0	Jackson, Smith
06/05/78	Aberdeen	N	SCF	2-1	MacDonald, Johnstone

Competition abbreviations

TC   Tennent Caledonian Cup
PD   Premier Division
ECWC   European Cup Winners' Cup
LC   League Cup
GC   Glasgow Cup
SC   Scottish Cup
LCF   League Cup Final
TEST   Testimonial
SCF   Scottish Cup Final
* After extra time
** Won 4-3 on penalties

FULL 1977/78 COMPETITIVE RESULTS AND PLAYER STATISTICS

APPEARANCES

	TC	PD	ECWC	LC	SC	GC	TEST	Total
Alex MacDonald	2	34	3	7	5	1	1	**53**
Alex Miller	2	16 (8)	2 (1)	5 (2)	1 (1)	1	0	**27 (12)**
Ally Dawson	0	1 (1)	0	0	0	0	0	**1 (1)**
Billy Mackay	0	1	(1)	1	0	1	0	**3 (1)**
Bobby McKean	2	6 (4)	2 (1)	1 (2)	0	(1)	0	**11 (8)**
Bobby Russell	2	33	4	7	4	1	1	**52**
Chris Robertson	(1)	2 (1)	1	0	0	0	0	**3 (2)**
Colin Jackson	0	35	4	7	5	1	1	**53**
Davie Cooper	2	34 (1)	4	8	5	1	1	**55 (1)**
Derek Johnstone	0	33	1	8	5	1	1	**49**
Derek Parlane	2	6 (13)	2	1 (3)	(2)	0	0	**11 (18)**
Derek Strickland	0	0	0	0	0	0	(1)	**(1)**
Eric Morris	0	0	0	0	(1)	0	0	**(1)**
Gordon Smith	0	34 (1)	3 (1)	8	5	0	1	**51 (2)**
John Greig	2	28 (1)	2	7	5	1	1	**46 (1)**
Johnny Hamilton	(1)	3 (1)	0	1	1	0	0	**5 (2)**
Kenny Watson	0	2 (2)	1	1 (1)	(1)	0	(1)	**4 (5)**
Martin Henderson	0	0	1	(1)	0	0	0	**1 (1)**
Peter McCloy	2	14	3	2	2	0	1	**24**
Sandy Jardine	2	32	4	8	5	0	1	**52**
Stewart Kennedy	0	22	1	6	3	1	0	**33**
Tom Forsyth	2	29	4	7	4	1	1	**48**
Tommy McLean	2	29 (2)	2	6	5	1	1	**46 (2)**

Figures in brackets represent substitute appearances

GOALS

	TC	PD	ECWC	LC	SC	GC	TEST	**Total**
Alex MacDonald	1	3	0	2	2	0	0	**8**
Alex Miller	0	2	0	3	0	0	0	**5**
Bobby Russell	0	3	0	0	0	0	2	**5**
Colin Jackson	0	3	0	1	2	0	0	**6**
Davie Cooper	1	6	0	1	1	0	0	**9**
Derek Johnstone	0	25	1	6	6	0	1	**39**
Derek Parlane	1	5	0	3	0	0	0	**9**
Gordon Smith	0	20	1	6	0	0	0	**27**
John Greig	0	2	1	1	1	0	2	**7**
Johnny Hamilton	0	0	0	0	1	0	0	**1**
Sandy Jardine	0	5	0	1	0	0	0	**6**
Tom Forsyth	0	0	0	0	0	1	0	**1**
Tommy McLean	0	1	0	2	0	1	0	**4**